POWER IN THE PIVOT

Your Roadmap to Finding a New Path

TEESHA CARTER

Freiling Agency

Power in the Pivot: Your Roadmap to Finding a New Path

Freiling Agency | www.freilingagency.com

PB ISBN: 978-1-969826-70-2

This book is dedicated to my mother, Gloria "Bird" Robertson Gary, my angel on earth and now my angel in heaven. Her love, beauty, strength, virtue, generosity, and unwavering care shaped my heart and my life. Everything good in me carries a piece of her. If I am even half the woman she was, then I know I have done well.

Forever loved. Forever missed. Forever with me.

CONTENTS

ONE

THE CALL YOU CAN'T IGNORE

Why Your Restlessness Is Actually Your Roadmap

You know that feeling when you've checked all the boxes—done everything you were supposed to do, achieved what you set out to achieve—but something still feels off?

Maybe you earned the degree your guidance counselor recommended. You landed the stable job your parents dreamed of for you. You're in a relationship that looks good on paper. You've built the life that everyone told you would make you happy. And yet, there you are at 3 AM, staring at the ceiling, wondering: Is this it?

Here's what I need you to understand right now: that restlessness you're feeling? It's not a problem. It's a roadmap.

THE BOXES THAT DON'T FIT

When I turned eighteen, I thought I had my entire life figured out. I was going to be a social worker, help children get out of abusive homes, make a real difference in the world. Growing up, I watched my mother—an actual angel on earth—serve everyone around her. We had foster children in our home. I was raised in a community of service, surrounded by people who gave their last dollar to anyone in need.

So naturally, I thought: Go to college, get a good degree, land a good job, and you'll be set for life. Money didn't matter to me at eighteen. Purpose did.

I got my bachelor's degree in sociology. I started working with people who needed a hand. I managed a homeless shelter. I became a case manager working with children and families dealing with severe mental illness. And you know what? I absolutely loved it. It was fulfilling work. Meaningful work. Important work.

But here's the thing about living: you learn yourself through the experience of it.

You don't know what you don't know until you try it. You don't discover who you're meant to become by staying in one place, doing one thing, checking one box. You discover it by living, by paying attention to those nudges in your spirit that say, "This was good, but it's not forever."

Give yourself permission to hear that voice. Because beating yourself up for not having everything figured out at eighteen—or twenty-eight, or thirty-eight—is a waste of precious energy. You didn't fail because your path changed. You grew because you were brave enough to let it.

WHEN GOD SENDS A TOW TRUCK

I'll never forget the day my car got towed.

I was nine months pregnant—and I mean ready-to-pop, carrying what would turn out to be a nine-pound baby. I was training a new case manager, and we went to visit a client in a community I'd never been to before. It was an initial assessment, so I had no idea the complex required a parking pass.

We were inside for maybe an hour. When we walked back outside, my trailblazer was gone. Just... gone.

At first, I thought maybe I was losing my mind. But the woman I was training looked at me with the same confused expression, and I knew: we definitely parked here. Turns out, my car had been towed. In less than an hour. And it was going to cost me eighty-five dollars to get it back.

Now, I could tell you this story and focus on the frustration, the inconvenience, the absurdity of the whole situation. But what I learned that day—standing there, nine months pregnant, car-less—was that sometimes God sends you signals you can't ignore.

I had already been feeling antsy in that position. I'd been there a little over three years, which for me is the sweet spot for restlessness. I'm the kind of person who goes in, assesses the situation, implements changes, and then starts looking for the next challenge. That's just how I'm wired. But I kept ignoring that inner voice because I was supposed to be grateful. I was supposed to stay put. This was good, meaningful work. Who leaves a job like that?

But that day, standing in that parking lot with my car nowhere in sight and a newborn on the way, I got the message loud and clear: It's time to move.

THE NUDGES YOU'VE BEEN IGNORING

Here's what I've learned about how God speaks to us: He starts with gentle nudges.

He'll speak to you through what you're reading, through conversations with friends, through sermons at church, through that quiet voice you hear when you finally sit still long enough to listen. He knows who you are. He knows what you need. And He knew what you were going to do before you even did it.

So when you're on a path that's different from what He has for you, He'll nudge you. Gently at first. Then a little harder. And if you keep ignoring Him? Well, sometimes He sends a tow truck.

That restlessness you're feeling—that sense that there's something more, something different, something calling you forward—that's not anxiety. That's not ingratitude. That's not you being difficult or unrealistic or unable to be satisfied with a good thing.

That's divine discontent. And it's trying to tell you something.

THE THREE STEPS THAT CHANGE EVERYTHING

After my car got towed, I knew I couldn't ignore the signs anymore. But knowing you need to make a change and actually making it are two very different things. So I developed a framework that has guided every major decision I've made since then. It's simple, but it's powerful:

Pray. Prepare. Pivot.

First, you pray. You nurture your relationship with God. You ask Him directly: What do you have for me? Who do you want me to impact? Who are you calling me to serve? Because here's the truth: in whatever field we work in, we are servants. Medical professionals serve. Politicians serve. Salespeople serve. We're all trying to meet someone's need, solve someone's problem, make someone's life better.

But you can't know who you're meant to serve without asking the One who designed you for that purpose.

Once you're clear on what God is telling you—and trust me, you'll know when it's Him—then you prepare. What does this next step require? Do you need more education? A certification? Do you need to update your resume and start applying? Do you need to change how you're showing up in the job you already have?

Maybe the call isn't to change your career at all. Maybe it's to become a changemaker in your family. A curse-breaker in your lineage. A leader in your community or church.

Whatever it is, preparation is where faith meets action. You can't just sit around thinking about it. You have to actually do something.

And then—here's the part that scares people—you pivot.

You make the change. You take the step. You do the thing that doesn't make sense to everyone else because it makes perfect sense to you and God.

FROM CASE MANAGER TO STATE EMPLOYEE TO... WHAT'S NEXT?

After that car-towing incident, I prayed. I prepared. And then I pivoted.

I left my position as a case manager and took a job with the state of Virginia, adjudicating disability claims. Now, if you'd asked me at eighteen if I wanted to spend my days analyzing medical documentation and making decisions about disability benefits, I would have said absolutely not. That wasn't the dream. That wasn't the plan.

But here's what I didn't realize then: God was preparing me.

Working in that position taught me about the human body in ways my social work background never could. I learned about the medical side of things—how physical health impacts mental health, how chronic conditions affect people's ability to work and live and function. I had already understood the emotional and mental aspects of human suffering from my previous roles. Now I was getting the full picture.

And guess what? Years later, when I moved into human resources and eventually into leadership coaching and consulting, that comprehensive understanding of people —body, mind, and spirit—became one of my greatest assets.

But I couldn't have known that at the time. I just knew it was time to go. And I trusted that if I took the step, God would show me why.

I stayed in that state position for nearly three years. And then—you guessed it—I got antsy again. The work that once intrigued me became routine. I was bored. And boredom, for me, is a sign that I'm no longer growing. And if I'm not growing, I'm not serving at my highest level.

So I prayed. I prepared. I pivoted.

I left the state job and took a position as a regional manager for a blood center. I implemented changes. I made an impact. And then it was time to move again.

Each time I made one of these moves, people questioned me. Family members worried. Friends didn't understand. "You're leaving a government job? Are you sure? What about security? What about benefits? What about staying put and being grateful for what you have?"

But here's what they didn't understand: staying in a position that no longer serves you isn't security. It's slow death.

THE PERMISSION YOU'VE BEEN WAITING FOR

Let me give you permission for something right now: Your path is allowed to change.

You're allowed to want something different at thirty-five than you wanted at eighteen. You're allowed to outgrow jobs, careers, even entire industries. You're allowed to discover that the thing you thought would fulfill you doesn't, and the thing you never considered might be exactly what your soul needs.

You're allowed to be the first person in your family to do something different. To break the mold. To try and fail and try again.

Because here's what I've learned from two decades of helping people transform their lives: the people who stay stuck aren't the ones who made mistakes. They're the ones who were too afraid to pivot when they felt the nudge.

Every single person I've worked with who feels trapped in their career can point to a moment—sometimes years ago—when they knew it was time to go. They felt the restlessness. They heard the call. But they talked themselves out of it. They convinced themselves to be grateful, to stay put, to ignore that voice whispering, "There's something more."

And now they're sitting in my office, twenty years later, wondering how their life became a prison instead of a purpose.

Don't let that be you.

YOUR RESTLESSNESS IS INFORMATION

The signs are everywhere. You just haven't been trained to see them.

That job that used to excite you now makes you sit in your car in the parking lot, gathering courage to walk inside. That relationship that once energized you now leaves you feeling drained. That dream you had five years ago keeps showing up in quiet moments, tapping on your shoulder, refusing to be ignored.

Your body is trying to tell you something. It's time to listen.

In my twenty years of HR work, I've conducted thousands of exit interviews. And I can tell you with absolute certainty: the number one reason people leave isn't money or benefits. It's not bad bosses or difficult coworkers or lack of advancement opportunities.

It's the growing gap between who they are and what they're being asked to do every single day.

They describe a restlessness. A knowing that they're meant for something more. A sense that they're operating at 50 percent capacity while their real gifts gather dust in a corner somewhere.

What most people don't realize is that this restlessness isn't a problem to solve. It's not something to medicate or ignore or push through. It's a compass. And it's pointing you toward your calling.

The question is: Are you going to follow it?

WHEN IT'S GOD, YOU KNOW

People often ask me, "How do you know when it's God calling you versus just your own restlessness or dissatisfaction?"

Here's my answer: When it's God, you know.

You feel it in your spirit. It won't leave you alone. It keeps showing up in different forms—a conversation, a sermon, a book, a moment of stillness where the message is so clear you can't deny it.

And here's the other thing about divine calls: they usually don't make logical sense. They don't fit neatly into your five-year plan. They often require you to do things that look crazy to everyone around you.

But when you're clear that it's God—when you've prayed about it, when you've studied His word, when you've surrounded yourself with like-minded people who help you discern His voice—then you have to be willing to move.

Quickly.

Because if you think too much about it, you'll talk yourself out of it. If you wait until you feel ready, you'll never start. If you need everyone's approval and understanding before you take the leap, you'll stay stuck forever.

Remember: God didn't give your calling to your mom, your dad, your spouse, or your best friend. He gave it to you. And yes, it will be lonely sometimes. Yes, people will question you. Yes, you'll doubt yourself.

But you'll also discover that there's a peace that comes from living in alignment with your purpose that no amount of external validation can provide.

THE ROADMAP IS ALREADY IN YOUR HANDS

Here's what I need you to understand before we go any further: Your restlessness isn't random. It's not a character flaw or a sign that something's wrong with you.

It's a roadmap.

Every time you've felt that nudge to do something different, try something new, walk away from something that no longer serves you—that was divine direction. Every moment you've sat in your car, not wanting to go into work or go home, not wanting to show up for one more obligation that drains you—that was information.

Your soul has been trying to tell you something. It's been leaving breadcrumbs, whispering directions, pointing you toward the life you're actually meant to live.

The only question now is: What are you going to do about it?

Are you going to keep ignoring the signs? Keep pushing down that restlessness? Keep convincing yourself to be grateful for a life that's killing your spirit?

Or are you going to do what Peter did when Jesus called him to walk on water?

You're going to take the step.

You're going to pray, prepare, and pivot.

You're going to trust that if God did it before, He'll do it again.

Because that's what this whole book is about: teaching you how to recognize the call, honor the restlessness, and take the leap that changes everything.

Your roadmap is already in your hands. It's been there all along, written in the language of divine discontent, holy restlessness, and that persistent whisper that says, "There's something more."

It's time to follow it.

REFLECTION QUESTIONS

1. What area of your life currently feels like you're "going through the motions" rather than living with purpose?
2. When was the last time you felt that nudge to make a change? What did you do with it?
3. If you could rewrite one chapter of your story without fear of judgment or failure, what would you change?
4. Who in your life needs your permission to change, grow, or pivot? (Hint: It might be you.)
5. What's one small step you could take this week to honor your restlessness instead of ignoring it?

TWO

THE SAFETY TRAP

How Staying Comfortable Is the Riskiest Choice You'll Ever Make

---

Let me paint you a picture.

You're sitting in your car in the parking lot at work. You've been here for ten minutes already, but you can't bring yourself to go inside. You check your phone. You adjust your rearview mirror. You take another sip of coffee that's already gotten cold.

At the end of the day, you do the same thing in your driveway at home. Sitting there, engine off, staring at your front door, gathering the energy to walk inside and be present for the people you love.

You've got the executive title. The impressive salary. The benefits package everyone said you should never walk away from. You've overcommitted yourself to this organization and that committee, thinking these extra responsibilities would give you more purpose, more fulfillment, more... something.

Instead, you feel overwhelmed. And empty.

Here's what I need you to hear: That feeling isn't a sign that something's wrong with you. It's a sign that you're living outside of your purpose. And the "safe" choices that got you here? They might be the most dangerous decisions you ever made.

THE SUCCESS THAT FEELS LIKE FAILURE

After two decades of working in HR and leadership development, I've seen this pattern play out hundreds of times. I call it the Golden Handcuffs Syndrome.

It happens when your achievements become the very chains that keep you from your calling.

You've climbed the ladder. You've earned the degrees. You've secured the position with the retirement plan and the health insurance and the three weeks of vacation time. On paper, you've made it. You've done everything your parents dreamed you would do, everything your professors said would lead to success, everything society tells you represents "having arrived."

But here's the trap: You're so afraid of losing what you've gained that you can't move toward what you're meant to gain.

I've watched brilliant executives stay in soul-crushing roles because the benefits were too good to walk away from. I've seen talented leaders plateau at positions that bore them senseless because leaving would mean starting over somewhere else. I've conducted exit interviews with people who waited twenty years too long to make the change they knew they needed to make, and the regret in their voices still haunts me.

You know what's wild? The research backs this up. Disengaged employees—people who show up but aren't really present, who do the work but don't bring their full selves to it—are 18 percent less productive and 12 percent less profitable than their engaged counterparts.

Your "safe" choice isn't just killing you. It's killing your impact.

THE BOAT WE'RE AFRAID TO LEAVE

There's a story in Scripture that always gets me. Peter walking on water. Jesus calls him out of the boat, and Peter actually does it—he steps out onto the waves. But then he looks around, realizes what he's doing, gets scared, and starts to sink.

We love to talk about Peter's lack of faith in that moment. But can we talk about the fact that he's the only one who got out of the boat in the first place?

While everyone else stayed safe and dry, Peter experienced something miraculous. Yes, he wavered. Yes, he doubted. But he also walked on water. Even if it was just for a few steps, he did what seemed impossible.

Here's my question for you: What boat are you refusing to leave?

Faith calls us to step out onto the waves. But our culture worships the boat. We've been conditioned to believe that security comes from external structures—the job, the title, the paycheck, the 401(k), the corner office with the window view.

But real security? Real security comes from knowing who you are and Whose you are.

When you understand that your identity isn't tied to your position, you're free to pursue your purpose. When you know that God has called you to something, you can trust Him to provide what you need to do it. When you're clear that your worth doesn't come from your achievements, you can risk leaving achievements behind to chase something greater.

The boat feels safe. But it's also limiting. And sometimes, the most dangerous thing you can do is stay where you are.

NOW WHAT?

I hit this wall myself a few years ago.

My two boys were grown—well, one was 24 and already out working and providing for his family, and the other had just graduated high school at 18. My husband and I were coming up on twenty years of marriage. We'd built a good life. A stable life. A successful life by every conventional measure.

And I remember sitting there one day thinking: Now what?

The kids didn't need me the way they used to. My career was solid but predictable. I'd spent years climbing ladders and checking boxes, and suddenly I was at the top looking around wondering why the view felt so... empty.

That's when I heard it. That quiet voice in my spirit, the one you can only hear when you stop moving long enough to listen: It's time to go. It's time to take on the world. It's time to travel more.

Now, I could have ignored that voice. I could have told myself to be grateful for the stability I had. I could have reminded myself that people don't just walk away from good government jobs with excellent benefits and retirement plans.

But here's what I've learned: When God says it's time to go, staying put is the riskiest choice you can make.

FIFTY STATES BY FIFTY

You know what I did instead? I made myself a promise: I was going to visit fifty states by the time I turned fifty.

Most people didn't understand it. "Why would you want to go to some of those states?" they'd ask. "What's in North Dakota? What are you going to do in Wyoming?"

But here's what they were missing: It wasn't about the destinations. It was about the expansion.

I wanted to see something different. Experience something different. Have a greater impact than I could have by staying comfortable in my familiar corner of the world.

Every state I visit teaches me something new. Every conversation with someone whose life looks nothing like mine stretches me. Every landscape I've never seen before reminds me that God's creation is so much bigger than my small, safe world.

And you know what? That decision to push past comfortable—to invest in experiences rather than just security—has been one of the most mind-opening, soul-expanding choices I've ever made.

But it required me to see that the real risk wasn't in going. The real risk was in staying.

THE INVISIBLE HANDCUFFS

This is what I mean by the safety trap. It's not just about jobs and careers. It's about every area of life where we choose comfort over calling, where we pick familiar over fulfilling, where we stay small because expanding feels too risky.

Those invisible handcuffs come in many forms:

The need for external approval. "What will people think if I leave this job? What will my parents say if I change careers? What will my colleagues think if I admit I'm not happy?"

The fear of looking like a beginner. "I'm too old to start over. I'm too educated to not have it all figured out. I'm too successful to go back to square one in a new field."

The worship of stability. "At least I know what I have here. At least the paycheck is guaranteed. At least I can predict what tomorrow will look like."

The comparison trap. "Everyone else seems satisfied with this level of success. Maybe I'm just being ungrateful. Maybe I should just learn to be content with what I have."

But here's the truth that nobody tells you: Age should not affect your purpose. Time constraints should not affect your purpose. What other people say should not affect your purpose.

Your purpose is between you and God. Period.

WHEN SUCCESS BECOMES A PRISON

In my HR work, I've seen this pattern most clearly in what I call the "successful and stuck" demographic. These are people who've achieved everything they set out to achieve —and now they're trapped by their own success.

They can't pivot to a new industry because they'd have to take a pay cut. They can't explore a different role because they've built their reputation in this one. They can't take a risk on their dream because they have responsibilities, obligations, people depending on them.

So they stay. They show up. They do the work. And they die a little bit inside every single day.

The irony? Their performance suffers. Their creativity dries up. Their leadership becomes transactional instead of transformational. They become the very definition of disengaged employees—going through the motions while their real gifts gather dust.

And the organization suffers too. Because mediocre effort from people operating at half-capacity will never produce the results that come from people operating in their purpose.

Everybody loses when you play it safe.

IT'S OKAY TO CHANGE AND GROW

Let me give you permission for something: It's okay to change and grow. It's okay to discover that the thing that fulfilled you five years ago doesn't fulfill you today. It's okay to realize that the title you worked so hard to earn doesn't fit who you're becoming.

Just because something was right for a season doesn't mean it's right forever.

When people questioned my decision to leave stable positions, to turn down opportunities that looked good on paper, to walk away from "sure things" in favor of uncertain callings, I had to remind myself: This may look like a step back to them, but it's actually a step toward what God is calling me to do.

The titles don't matter as much as we think they do. The accolades feel good, but they're not the point. The corner office and the parking spot and the name on the door—

none of that compares to the feeling of waking up excited about your purpose.

Until you align your work with your calling, you will be depleted and unhappy. I don't care how impressive your resume is. I don't care how much money you make. I don't care how many people tell you how lucky you are to have what you have.

If you're living outside your purpose, you're slowly suffocating. And all the success in the world won't give you the oxygen you need to breathe.

THE STEP THAT SEEMS IMPOSSIBLE

So what does this mean practically?

Maybe it means going back to school later in life to expand your education. Maybe it means taking up a skill or trade you've always wanted to learn. Maybe it means finally admitting that the career path you've been on isn't the one you want to stay on.

Maybe it means taking swimming lessons at forty. Maybe it means planning a trip that scares you. Maybe it means having an honest conversation with your spouse about the fact that you're not happy, even though on paper everything looks perfect.

Maybe it means breaking away from unreasonable expectations—the idea that achievement and success have to look a certain way. Maybe it means recognizing that there are times of pivot in life, and you have to be willing to do something different to fully live the life God has for you.

Whatever it is, I can promise you this: It will feel uncomfortable. It will look risky. It will require you to be willing to be a beginner again, to feel uncertain, to face the possibility that it might not work out exactly the way you planned.

But staying where you are—in the job that's draining you, in the pattern that's limiting you, in the comfortable prison of other people's expectations—that's the riskiest choice of all.

Because time is the one resource you can never get back. And every day you spend living outside your purpose is a day you can't reclaim.

THE REAL DEFINITION OF SECURITY

Here's what I've come to understand about security: It's not about having a guaranteed paycheck or a stable job or a predictable future.

Real security is knowing that you're walking in your purpose. Real security is trusting that the God who called you to something will equip you to do it. Real security is believing that your gifts and talents will make room for you, regardless of what title you hold or what company employs you.

When you operate from that place—when you understand that you're a valuable business asset, that opportunities abound, that your worth isn't tied to your current position—you're free.

Free to take risks. Free to pursue callings. Free to leave behind what no longer serves you. Free to step out of the boat and walk on water, even if only for a few steps.

The Golden Handcuffs only work if you believe the lie that you need them. But once you realize that your security comes from who you are and Whose you are, not from what you've achieved or accumulated?

Those handcuffs fall right off.

THE INVITATION

So here's my challenge to you: Take off the handcuffs.

Stop letting external definitions of success dictate your choices. Stop worrying so much about what other people will think. Stop sacrificing your purpose on the altar of stability.

Take the swimming lessons. Book the trip. Have the conversation. Explore the possibility. Take the step that everyone else thinks is crazy but you know in your gut is exactly right.

Because playing it safe might protect you from failure, but it will also prevent you from flying.

And you weren't created to spend your whole life in the boat. You were created to walk on water.

The waves are waiting. What are you so afraid of?

REFLECTION QUESTIONS

1. What "golden handcuffs" are currently keeping you from pursuing your purpose? (Be specific: Is it salary? Benefits? Fear of judgment? Something else?)

2. If you removed external definitions of success from the equation, what would you be doing with your life right now?

3. What's one area where you've been choosing comfort over calling? What's that choice costing you?

4. What would it look like to "take swimming lessons" in your life—to pursue something you've always wanted to learn or experience, regardless of your age or current life stage?

5. When you think about stepping out of your current "boat," what are you actually afraid will happen? Write down your worst-case scenario, then ask yourself: Is that fear bigger than my calling?

THREE

THE 5-SECOND LEAP

The Moment Between Knowing and Doing

There's a split second between inspiration and hesitation. Between "yes" and "but what if?" Between hearing God's voice and drowning it out with your own anxious thoughts.

Five seconds. That's all it takes for your brain to kill a God-given idea with overthinking.

You get the nudge: Apply for that position. Start that business. Have that difficult conversation. Make that call. Book that trip.

And then your mind kicks into overdrive: But I'm not ready. But what about the cost. But what will people think. But I need to research more. But I need a plan. But, but, but...

Here's what I've learned after two decades of watching people either take the leap or talk themselves out of it: The difference between those who succeed and those who stay stuck isn't talent, education, or resources.

It's the willingness to move in that five-second window before fear has a chance to build its case.

THE PERFECTIONISM TRAP

Let me tell you what perfectionism really is: It's fear wearing a productivity costume.

We tell ourselves we're being responsible, strategic, careful. We convince ourselves that we just need a little more time to prepare, a few more details nailed down, one more certification, another conversation, a clearer sign.

But what we're really doing is stalling. We're waiting for a level of certainty that will never come. We're trying to eliminate all risk before we take the risk, which is like trying to learn to swim without getting in the water.

Most of the time, perfectionism isn't about excellence. It's about control. And underneath control is fear—fear of failing, fear of looking foolish, fear of disappointing others, fear of discovering we're not as capable as we thought.

But here's what perfectionism costs you: opportunity.

While you're over there perfecting your plan, someone else with 70 percent of your talent and 40 percent of your preparation is already doing the thing. They're learning on the job. They're adjusting as they go. They're building momentum while you're still color-coding your spreadsheet.

And you know what? Businesses that have been running successfully for years are still figuring it out. There are companies generating millions in revenue that don't have it all straight. There are leaders at the top of their industries who are making decisions without perfect information.

Because here's the secret: You don't need to have it all figured out. You just need to be willing to start.

WHEN GOD SAYS GO

In 2025, my motto was "Teesha Takes the World." My plan was to travel internationally, speak on stages around the globe, continue visiting all fifty states by fifty. I had my vision board. I had my goals. I had my perfectly organized plan.

And then God showed me—like He always does—that His plans are bigger than mine.

Every year, my church does a mission trip. And every year, I listen to the announcement and keep it moving. Mission trips weren't really my thing. I had my reasons: I'm a hotel snob. I like what I like. I don't like bugs. I'm a pescatarian, so I only eat certain things.

The whole idea of a mission trip meant discomfort. It meant giving up control. It meant putting myself in situations that were designed to serve others, not to make me comfortable.

But this particular year, when they played that announcement, something hit different.

The screen said "Leadership Training." And I felt that nudge. That unmistakable knowing that this was for me.

Immediately, the questions flooded in: What about the bugs? What about the accommodations? What if I don't know anyone in the group? What will the food situation be? What about—

I could feel myself spiraling. So you know what I did?

I sent an email to the director that exact same day. It was a Sunday. I asked all my questions—every single one. And when she wrote back with answers, I signed up immediately.

Not the next day. Not after I thought about it more. Not after I talked to five more people and made a pros-and-cons list.

Immediately.

Because I knew if I gave myself time to think, I would talk myself out of it. And I couldn't let fear disguised as "being practical" steal what God was clearly calling me to do.

THE TRIP THAT CHANGED EVERYTHING

That mission trip to Nairobi, Kenya became one of the most transformative experiences of my life.

Let me tell you what happened: My husband went with me. This man who had been wanting to go to Africa his entire life but had never made it happen. We'd talked about it. We'd even said we'd go this year. But we never actually planned it because it was expensive, complicated, and we couldn't figure out the perfect time to go.

Until God provided the opportunity. And we took it. Immediately.

The experience was everything I feared—and nothing like I expected. Yes, there were bugs. Yes, the accommodations weren't the Ritz-Carlton. Yes, I had to get creative with my eating preferences.

But the children we met. The leaders we trained. The emerging leaders who were so hungry for knowledge and encouragement. The gratitude radiating from every person we encountered. The spiritual growth my husband and I experienced together.

He talked about vulnerability in ways he never had before. We had conversations about faith and purpose that went deeper than twenty years of marriage had taken us. I watched him transform in real-time, and he watched me step into a calling I didn't even know I had.

I will never be the same. And I can't wait to go back.

But here's the thing: None of that would have happened if I'd given myself time to think about it. If I'd waited until I felt ready. If I'd let my need for comfort override my call to serve.

What if I had talked myself out of it? What if I had let the bugs and the tents and the uncertainty win?

I would have missed one of the most profound experiences of my life. And so would my husband. And so would every person we were meant to touch on that trip.

That's what's at stake when you let overthinking kill your God-given ideas.

SEVEN DAYS TO FOREVER

You want to know another time I moved quickly? When I met my husband.

Now, we'd known each other years before—he was close friends with one of my cousins. But we'd lost touch. Then in October 2005, he came to Virginia to visit, and we reconnected.

October 3rd, we met. By October 10th—seven days later—he told me he loved me. By January, he proposed. By August, we were married.

Seven. Days.

Most people thought we were crazy. "You need to get to know each other better," they said. "What's the rush? Why not take your time?"

But here's what I knew: He was exactly what I had prayed for. And he later told me I was exactly what he wanted. So why prolong it? Why pretend we needed more time to be sure when we were already sure?

We're coming up on twenty years of marriage now. Twenty years. And you know what I tell people when they ask how we made it work?

When you know, you know. And when God confirms it, you move.

We didn't have all the answers. We didn't have a perfect plan. We didn't know how every detail would work out. We just knew we were supposed to be together, and we trusted God to fill in the blanks.

That's what faith looks like in action. It's not about having perfect clarity. It's about having conviction and choosing to act on it.

THE FAITH-ACTION BRIDGE

In my work with leaders and organizations, I've discovered something powerful: Successful transitions don't happen through grand gestures of bravery. They happen in micro-moments of courage.

I call it the "Faith-Action Bridge." It's that five-second window where you can either take the step or talk yourself out of it. Where you can either trust what you know in your spirit or give in to what your fear is screaming in your head.

Here's how it works practically:

You get the nudge. The idea. The knowing. That moment where God is clearly showing you the next step.

You have five seconds to act on it before your logical mind takes over and starts building arguments against it.

In those five seconds, you:

Acknowledge the nudge ("I hear you, God")

Make the smallest possible commitment ("I'm going to send that email right now")

Take immediate action before fear catches up ("Submit button: clicked")

That's it. Five seconds. One small action. Momentum created.

Because here's the thing about momentum: Once you've taken the first step, the second step gets easier. Once you've made the initial commitment, backing out feels harder than moving forward. Once you've told people what you're doing, accountability keeps you going even when doubt creeps in.

The five-second leap isn't about being reckless. It's about not letting overthinking kill what God has already confirmed.

DISTINGUISHING BETWEEN GOD'S TIMING AND FEAR'S DELAYS

Now, I know what some of you are thinking: "But Teesha, how do I know if I'm supposed to wait or if I'm just being afraid?"

Great question. And it's one I've wrestled with many times.

Here's how I distinguish between God's timing and fear-based delays:

God's timing comes with peace, even when the wait is frustrating. Fear-based delays come with anxiety and a sense that you're slowly dying inside.

God's timing usually involves active preparation—learning, connecting, building. Fear-based delays involve endless research that never leads to action.

God's timing has a "not yet, but soon" quality. Fear-based delays feel like "never, because it's impossible."

God's timing often involves waiting for confirmation, open doors, or aligned circumstances. Fear-based delays involve moving the goalposts every time you get close to being ready.

When God is asking you to wait, you'll feel like you're being prepared. When fear is making you wait, you'll feel like you're being paralyzed.

There's a difference between due diligence and decision paralysis. There's a difference between wise planning and perfectionist procrastination. There's a difference between trusting God's timing and using "God's timing" as an excuse to stay comfortable.

And deep down, you know which one you're dealing with.

BIBLICAL URGENCY

You know what I love about Scripture? God repeatedly emphasizes the importance of moving quickly when He calls.

Think about the day of Pentecost—the Holy Spirit came rushing in suddenly, and everybody had to move quickly to respond. There was no "let me think about this for a few months and get back to you."

Or consider when Jesus told Judas, "What you are about to do, do quickly." Jesus knew that overthinking leads to hesitation, and hesitation gives fear time to build its case.

Throughout the Bible, when God calls people to something, there's an urgency to it. Not a recklessness—but a knowing that delayed obedience is still disobedience.

God knows us. He knows that if we think too much about what He's asking, we'll talk ourselves out of it. We'll come up with a thousand logical reasons why it can't work, won't work, shouldn't work.

So He creates these moments where we have to choose: Trust what we know in our spirit, or listen to what we fear in our head.

The five-second leap is really about choosing faith over fear in that critical window before logic takes over.

WHEN ANXIETY SHOWS UP AFTER THE LEAP

Here's what I need you to know: Moving quickly doesn't mean you won't experience doubt afterward.

When I signed up for that Kenya trip immediately, you know what happened later? The anxiety hit. The "oh my goodness, what have I done?" The mental replay of all the reasons this was a terrible idea.

But here's the thing: I was already committed. I'd already signed up. The decision was made.

And that's actually the beauty of the five-second leap. When the anxiety comes—and it will come—you're already past the point of easy retreat. You've created momentum. You've made a commitment. You've put yourself in a position where moving forward is actually easier than backing out.

If I had given myself time to think about Kenya before signing up, I would have created a mental list of every possible thing that could go wrong. And that list would have convinced me to stay home.

But because I moved immediately, by the time the doubts showed up, I was already in. And now the question wasn't "Should I do this?" but rather "How am I going to prepare for this amazing thing I've committed to?"

See the difference? The five-second leap shifts your relationship with doubt. Instead of letting doubt prevent action, you use action to put doubt in its proper place.

THE BUSINESSES THAT ARE STILL FIGURING IT OUT

Let me tell you something that should relieve some pressure: Every successful business you admire is still figuring things out.

That company that's been operating for ten years? They're still learning. That entrepreneur who seems to have it all together? They're adjusting their strategy quarterly. That leader whose Instagram makes everything look perfect? They're troubleshooting problems you'll never see.

Nobody has it all figured out. Nobody starts with perfect systems and flawless execution. Nobody waits until they're 100 percent ready before they launch.

You learn by doing. You figure it out on the way. You adjust your approach based on real-world feedback, not theoretical perfection.

Some things you just don't know until you know. Some lessons can only be learned through experience. Some clarity only comes after you've taken the first step.

So stop waiting to have it all figured out. Stop thinking you need one more certification, one more conversation, one more sign before you move.

You have enough. You know enough. You are enough.

Now move.

THE COST OF HESITATION

I've watched too many talented people miss their moment because they hesitated too long.

They spent months analyzing the "perfect" time to make a career transition, only to watch the opportunity pass them by. They waited to feel ready to start the business, and someone else launched the same idea. They delayed having the important conversation until the relationship was too damaged to repair.

Hesitation has a price. And that price is often higher than the cost of moving before you feel completely ready.

Yes, there's wisdom in preparation. Yes, there's value in thoughtful planning. Yes, there's a place for counting the cost and considering the implications.

But there's also such a thing as analysis paralysis. There's such a thing as preparing so long that you never actually perform. There's such a thing as being so careful that you never actually live.

The most successful leaders I know aren't the ones who wait for perfect clarity. They're the ones who act on conviction even when the path isn't perfectly clear.

They take the five-second leap. And then they trust God to catch them.

TRUST HIM TO WORK IT OUT

Here's what I want you to understand: You're not jumping alone.

When you take that five-second leap, when you act on what God has shown you even though you don't have all the answers, you're not being reckless. You're being faithful.

You're trusting that the God who called you to something will equip you to do it. You're believing that His timing is perfect even when it feels premature to you. You're acknowledging that He knows exactly what He's doing, even when you don't.

We don't have all the answers anyway. We never will. Perfect clarity is a myth. Complete certainty is a fantasy.

But we can have faith. We can have conviction. We can have that knowing in our spirit that says, "This is it. This is the moment. This is what I'm supposed to do."

And when we have that? We move. Quickly. Before fear builds its case. Before doubt gets a vote. Before overthinking kills what God has already confirmed.

Trust Him to work it out. Trust Him to fill in the blanks. Trust Him to provide what you need when you need it. Trust His timing, even when it makes no logical sense.

Because that's what faith is: taking action on belief even when the ground beneath your feet feels uncertain.

THE INVITATION

So here's my challenge to you: Stop overthinking it.

That thing you've been praying about, researching, "waiting for clarity" on—you already know what you're supposed to do. You've already heard God's voice. You've already felt the nudge.

Now you just need to move. In the next five seconds. Before your brain talks you out of it.

Send the email. Make the call. Sign up for the thing. Book the ticket. Start the conversation. Submit the application.

Do it now. Not tomorrow. Not next week. Not when you feel more ready.

Now.

Because the difference between the life you're living and the life you're meant to live might be just five seconds of courage.

What are you waiting for?

REFLECTION QUESTIONS

1. What God-given idea have you been overthinking instead of acting on? What's one micro-action you could take in the next five seconds?

2. Think about a time you moved quickly on something God told you to do. What was the result? How would things be different if you'd hesitated?

3. What's the difference between wise preparation and fear-based delay in your current situation? Be honest with yourself.

4. What are you afraid will happen if you take the leap before you feel completely ready?

5. If you knew God would work out all the details, what would you do today?

FOUR

REWRITING YOUR STORY

From Survivor Mode to Changemaker Mode

Every single one of us is carrying a story. Not the story of what actually happened to us, but the story we tell ourselves about what it all means.

That story shapes everything. How we see opportunities. What we believe we deserve. Which risks feel reasonable and which feel reckless. Whether we think we're the kind of person who gets to live an extraordinary life or the kind who should just be grateful for ordinary.

For most of us, that story was written a long time ago. By parents who loved us and wanted to protect us. By teachers who meant well but had limited vision. By a culture that values safety over calling and survival over purpose.

And here's the hard truth: The story that once protected you might be the very thing that's now preventing your breakthrough.

But here's the good news: You're not stuck with that story. You can rewrite it. In real time. Starting today.

THE STORY I INHERITED

Let me tell you about the story I grew up with.

The people in my life—my family, teachers, guidance counselors, administrators—they gave me magnificent guidance. They taught me what they knew. They prepared me for the world as they understood it. And their intentions were beautiful.

But their vision was also limiting.

The story went like this: Go to college. Get a good job. If you can get a government job, even better. Stay there. Work hard. Be grateful. Don't ask for too much. Security comes from stability, and stability comes from staying put.

My parents were the perfect examples of this story. My mom worked at her job for thirty-seven years. My dad stayed at his for forty-one years. Same jobs. Same routine. Same paycheck for decades.

They were baby boomers, raised in a time when staying was everything. When loyalty to an employer was rewarded. When you got a job and you kept it, and that's how you built a life.

So when I started my career and felt antsy after just three years at a position, I thought something was wrong with me.

I'd go into an organization, assess what needed to change, implement new systems, see results, and then... I'd be bored. Ready for the next challenge. Restless in a way that felt like failure.

Because the story I'd inherited said: If you're leaving, you're not being loyal. If you're bored, you're being ungrateful. If you're looking for something more after just a few years, you're the problem.

But you know what I eventually realized? That story wasn't mine. It was theirs. And it served them beautifully in their generation, in their economy, in their season.

But I was living in a different season. And I needed a different story.

WHEN THE PROTECTOR BECOMES THE PRISON

Here's what I've learned from working with hundreds of leaders, from conducting thousands of exit interviews, from helping people transform their careers and their lives:

The story that protected your family can become the very thing that prevents your purpose.

Think about it. Your parents or grandparents might have developed a "keep your head down" mentality because it literally kept them safe. Maybe they lived through discrimination, economic hardship, or unstable times when drawing attention could be dangerous.

So they learned to survive. They mastered the art of making do, being grateful for what they had, not reaching for too much. And that story—that survivor mentality—saved them. It got them through. It protected them and you.

But now you're trying to thrive, not just survive. You're trying to step into a calling, not just keep a job. You're trying to break generational patterns, not repeat them.

And that old story? It's not helping anymore. It's holding you back.

I see this all the time in my work. High-achievers who have mastered the art of surviving and succeeding, but who have never learned to thrive in their true calling. They've climbed ladders—tall ones, impressive ones—

only to discover those ladders were leaning against the wrong walls.

They did everything "right" according to the story they inherited. They played it safe. They stayed grateful. They didn't ask for too much.

And now they're successful, secure, and slowly dying inside.

THE CHANGEMAKER AWAKENING

I'll never forget a conversation I had with someone close to me. We were talking about purpose and calling, and they asked a question that stopped me in my tracks:

"Did God love us just that much? That He picked out each individual person, gave us unique characteristics and unique traits, and He's going to use them for His glory and to advance us?"

Yes. The answer is yes.

God didn't create you to be a carbon copy of your parents or your community or the generation before you. He didn't give you unique gifts so you could file them away and follow someone else's script.

He created you to be a changemaker. And that means your story gets to be different.

But becoming a changemaker requires breaking away from the norm. Breaking away from what we know. Breaking away from what we do. And that's terrifying, especially when you're the first one in your family to do it.

When you're the one breaking generational curses. Exceeding expectations. Moving in excellence while everyone around you is asking, "Why can't you just be satisfied with good enough?"

THE LIMITS OF WELL-MEANING GUIDANCE

Here's what I need you to understand: When God tells you to do something, He tells you. Not your mom. Not your dad. Not your siblings. Not your best friend. Not even your spouse, usually.

Just you.

And that makes it really difficult to navigate. Because the people you love and trust, the ones who have guided you your whole life, they don't always see what God is showing you.

I remember the first time I quit a government job. I'd been working for the state of Virginia, adjudicating Social Security disability claims. It was a good job. Stable. The kind of position my parents would have stayed in for forty years.

But after nearly three years, I was bored. I'd learned what I needed to learn. I'd made the contribution I could make. I was no longer growing, and when I'm not growing, I'm dying.

So I quit.

And people couldn't understand it. "You're leaving a state job? Why would you do that? Do you know how many people would love to have that position?"

Yes, I knew. But I also knew it wasn't mine to keep anymore. It wasn't where God was calling me. And staying would have been choosing their story over mine.

THE PATTERN OF LEAVING

This became a pattern in my life. I'd get a position, excel at it, implement changes, see results, and then feel that familiar restlessness that meant it was time to move.

I became a regional manager for a blood center. Got promoted, did the work, made things better. And then it no longer served me. So I left.

I took an HR director position with a county government. Six figures. Great benefits. All the markers of success according to that inherited story. But I was no longer filled because it was outside of the purpose God had for me.

So I quit. Again.

And every time, people questioned me. Every time, my parents' voices echoed in my head: "You get a job and you stay. Why are you always leaving? Why can't you just be satisfied?"

But here's what I finally understood: I wasn't leaving because I was dissatisfied. I was leaving because I was being obedient.

God was calling me to consult. To speak. To train leaders. To have a bigger impact than one organization could contain. And I couldn't step into that calling while I was clinging to a job that fit someone else's story.

THE PLOT TWIST YOU DIDN'T SEE COMING

You want to know what happened after I quit that county HR director job?

One of my first consulting clients was the organization I'd just left.

I was able to work with them on a contract basis. I could still make an impact. I could still influence the progress I'd started. But now I had the freedom to serve multiple organizations, to expand my reach, to operate in the fullness of my purpose.

If I had stayed, if I had let fear or other people's stories keep me in that position, I never would have discovered that possibility. The opportunity didn't show up until I took the step.

Here's another example: A diversity, equity, and inclusion leadership opportunity came up at one of the county governments where I'd worked. At that time, I was crystal clear that I was supposed to be consulting, not going back into full-time employment.

They wanted someone full-time. I told them I could only consult. That didn't fit their model, so I didn't take the position.

Fast forward one year. You know what happened? The government eliminated many DEI initiatives. Those positions—including the one they wanted me to take full-time—disappeared.

If I had ignored what God was telling me, if I had gone against my calling because it fit better with the traditional story of employment, I could have been out of a job with no backup plan.

But because I listened? Because I chose to write my own story instead of following the script? I was protected. I was positioned. I was exactly where I needed to be.

THE GENERATIONS WATCHING

Here's what makes rewriting your story so important: It's not just about you.

Your story isn't just personal. It's generational.

The beliefs that limit you were often passed down like heirlooms—unexamined, unchallenged, assumed to be universal truths rather than one generation's survival strategies.

But when you break free from a limiting story, you don't just change your life. You change the trajectory for everyone who comes after you.

Think about it. If I had stayed stuck in that "get a job and never leave" mentality, what would I be teaching my sons? That security is more important than calling? That survival is the goal rather than purpose? That you should ignore God's voice if it conflicts with conventional wisdom?

No. I'm teaching them something different. I'm showing them that it's okay to follow where God leads, even when it looks risky to everyone else. I'm modeling what it means to rewrite limiting stories. I'm giving them permission to write their own stories instead of inheriting mine.

That's what changemakers do. We don't just survive. We transform. And in transforming, we make it possible for the next generation to start from a different place.

THE VALUABLE BUSINESS ASSET

Let me tell you something I had to learn: You are a valuable business asset.

Say it with me: I am a valuable business asset.

That means opportunities abound. If one position doesn't serve you anymore, you use what you've learned and go get what's next. If one organization can't contain your gifts, you find one that can—or you create your own.

This mindset is part of rewriting your story. The old story says: "Be grateful for what you have because there might not be anything else." The new story says: "I bring value wherever I go, and the right opportunities will find me because I'm walking in my purpose."

The old story says: "Don't rock the boat. Don't take risks. Stay where you're safe." The new story says: "I'm willing to trade security for calling because I know God will provide."

The old story says: "You failed if you had to leave." The new story says: "You succeeded at that chapter, and now it's time for the next one."

See the difference? Same circumstances, completely different interpretation.

THE COST OF STAYING IN THE OLD STORY

Let me be really clear about something: Not taking the step, not rewriting your story, doesn't keep you safe. It prevents you from living fully in what God has for you.

Sometimes staying stagnant—or worse, going against what God has clearly called you to do—turns out negatively.

I've seen it happen. People who ignore the nudge, who silence the restlessness, who choose the old story over the new calling. And years later, they're filled with regret. The "what ifs" haunt them. The opportunities they missed become the stories they can't stop telling.

Because here's the thing about survivor mode: It's designed to get you through crisis, not to help you build a legacy.

Survivors do what they have to do. Changemakers do what they're called to do. Survivors focus on not losing. Changemakers focus on fulfilling purpose.

And you can't live in both modes at the same time. You have to choose.

HONORING THE PAST WITHOUT BEING IMPRISONED BY IT

Now, I want to be clear about something: Rewriting your story doesn't mean dishonoring where you came from.

My parents' story wasn't wrong. It was right for them, for their time, for their circumstances. The stability they created gave me opportunities they never had. The security they built became the foundation I could launch from.

I honor that. I'm grateful for that. I wouldn't be who I am without the story they lived.

But honoring their story doesn't mean I have to live it. Respecting their choices doesn't mean I have to make the same ones. Being grateful for the foundation doesn't mean I have to stay in the basement.

You can honor your past while refusing to be imprisoned by it. You can acknowledge that old stories served their purpose while recognizing that new seasons require new narratives.

This is how you rewrite your story from a place of faith rather than fear. You don't reject everything that came before. You build on it. You learn from it. You take what was good and release what's limiting.

And then you write the next chapter in your own voice.

FROM SURVIVOR TO CHANGEMAKER

So what does this look like practically? How do you actually rewrite your story in real time?

First, you identify the limiting narrative. What's the story you've been telling yourself about why you can't have what you want? Why you can't pursue that calling? Why you can't make that change?

Is it: "People like me don't do things like that"? Is it: "I should just be grateful for what I have"? Is it: "Stability is the most important thing"? Is it: "I'm not the kind of person who takes big risks"?

Write it down. Name it. Look at it clearly.

Second, you ask yourself: Where did this story come from? Who wrote it? What was happening in their life that made this story necessary?

Often, you'll realize the story came from someone else's experience, someone else's fears, someone else's season. And it may have been exactly right for them. But it's not yours.

Third, you write a new story. Not a fantasy or a delusion, but a faith-based narrative that aligns with who God created you to be and what He's calling you to do.

The new story sounds like: "I am a changemaker in my family, and that's a calling, not a rebellion." Or: "God has given me unique gifts, and I honor Him by using them fully." Or: "I am a valuable business asset, and opportunities are abundant for those walking in their purpose."

Fourth, you live into the new story. You make decisions based on it. You speak from it. You let it guide your steps even when the old story screams at you to turn back.

And here's what happens: The more you live into the new story, the more true it becomes. The neural pathways in your brain literally rewire. The evidence accumulates. The confidence builds. And one day, you realize the old story doesn't even feel true anymore.

That's when you know you've become a changemaker.

THE INVITATION

So here's what I want you to know: You are not bound by your past. You are not limited by your family's story. You are not required to live out a script that someone else wrote for you, no matter how much they love you or how good their intentions were.

God gave you a unique set of gifts, experiences, and callings for a reason. And part of your purpose is to write a story that's worth passing down—not because it's perfect, but because it's true to who you are.

Will it be scary? Yes. Will people question you? Absolutely. Will you sometimes doubt yourself and wonder if the old story was safer? Of course.

But you'll also experience something the survivors never get to feel: the joy of living fully in your purpose. The freedom of walking in your calling. The peace that comes from obedience even when it doesn't make sense to anyone else.

You get to rewrite your story. You get to be the first one in your family to break the pattern. You get to be the changemaker that future generations will look back on and say, "That's when everything changed."

So pick up the pen. Start writing. Your story is waiting.

REFLECTION QUESTIONS

1. What's the limiting story you inherited about work, success, or what's possible for someone like you? Write it down in one sentence.

2. Who wrote that story originally? What was happening in their life that made that narrative necessary for them?

3. If you were to rewrite your story from a place of faith rather than fear, what would the new narrative say?

4. What decision would you make differently if you fully believed the new story instead of the old one?

5. Who in the next generation is watching you? What story do you want them to inherit from your life?

FIVE

THE COURAGE EQUATION

How to Build Bravery Like a Muscle

Here's what most people get wrong about courage: They think it's something you either have or you don't. Like it's a personality trait you're born with, a gene you either inherited or missed out on.

They see someone taking a bold leap and think, "Well, that's just who they are. They're naturally brave. I could never do that."

But let me tell you something I've learned after two decades of watching people transform their lives: Courage isn't something you're born with. It's something you build.

Like a muscle, courage grows stronger every time you use it. And like a muscle, it atrophies when you don't.

The question isn't whether you have courage. The question is whether you're willing to develop it.

THE COURAGE EQUATION

In my years of leadership development, I've discovered that courage follows a predictable pattern. It's not about the absence of fear—it's about the presence of something stronger than fear.

I call it the Courage Equation: Faith + Action + Community = Unstoppable Momentum.

Let me break that down.

Faith is believing that God has called you to something, even when you can't see the whole path. It's trusting that the One who created you also equipped you. It's knowing that if He did it before, He'll do it again.

Action is taking the step even when you're scared. It's doing the thing before you feel ready. It's moving on conviction rather than waiting for confidence.

Community is surrounding yourself with people who believe in your calling even when you're doubting it. It's having voices in your life that remind you who you are when fear tries to tell you who you're not.

When you combine these three elements, something powerful happens. You build momentum. And momentum makes the next step easier than the first one was.

This is how courage becomes a skill rather than a trait. This is how ordinary people do extraordinary things. Not because they're naturally brave, but because they've learned to build bravery systematically.

THE FIRST FAILED ATTEMPT

Let me tell you about the first time I tried to move to Atlanta. It was 2005—the year I met my husband.

He was living in Atlanta at the time, and from our very first conversation, we talked about the possibility of me relocating. This wasn't just some casual dating scenario. This was serious. This was "we're planning a future together" serious.

I quit my job in Virginia—the one where I was working as a case manager, the one I loved, the one where I was making a real impact. I gave notice on my apartment. I gave away all my furniture. I packed up a U-Haul with clothes and my son's things, and we moved.

I was pregnant at the time, by the way. And three months pregnant means I'd given up my health insurance when I left my job. Our wedding was scheduled for August 5th, 2006, so it wasn't going to be long without coverage, but still—it felt vulnerable. It felt risky.

It felt like faith in action.

I stayed in Atlanta for four days. And then I went back home.

Four. Days.

You want to know why? Because I hadn't yet developed the courage I needed. I did it scared, but I wasn't ready. I got sick—or at least that's the story I told myself. The truth is, I wasn't strong enough yet. I didn't have the spiritual muscle memory to sustain the leap.

My husband moved back to Virginia with me after we got married. And we stayed there. For years. Living in the familiar, the comfortable, the safe.

Until 2014.

WHEN GOD SAYS "ENLARGE YOUR TERRITORY"

By 2014, everything was different. My boys were older. My career was stable. My husband and I had built a good life in Virginia.

But I kept feeling that nudge. That restlessness. That knowing that there was something more waiting for me beyond the borders of my comfort zone.

I started praying specifically: "God, enlarge my territory." What I meant was that I wanted to meet more people, expand my network, increase my influence.

What God heard was: "I told you eight years ago it was time to move, and now you're finally ready to listen."

Things started happening. My husband was having some challenges at work. I was feeling ready—actually ready this time—for a change. We started applying for positions in Atlanta, Charlotte, and Richmond.

And then something shifted. I was sitting in church, and the preacher was talking about taking steps, about doing things quickly when God calls you, about not waiting until you feel ready.

I could feel it in my spirit—she was talking directly to me. Every word was confirmation. Every example hit home. It was like God was using her voice to remove every excuse I'd been holding onto.

THE DIFFERENCE EIGHT YEARS MAKES

On May 12, 2014, we moved to Cobb County, Georgia.

Same destination as 2006. Same dream. Same calling. But this time? I had built the courage I needed to sustain it.

This time, I had secured a position before moving. This time, my children were at a stable place in their lives. This time, I had surrounded myself with people who encouraged me to take the leap rather than questioned why I would leave something good.

This time, I didn't just have faith. I had faith plus action plus community.

And let me tell you—it has been the most amazing experience. I have never once considered moving back. In fact, I can't even imagine it. That's how much of a perfect fit this has been.

Since moving to Atlanta, I've started my own business. I've become an author. I've expanded my speaking and consulting in ways that never would have been possible if I'd stayed in Virginia. I travel back quarterly to visit, and I still love my home state, but I'm crystal clear that this is where I'm meant to be.

But here's the key insight: The same calling that failed in 2006 succeeded in 2014. Not because the calling changed, but because I changed. I had developed the courage muscle. I had learned that if God did it before, He'll do it again.

The first attempt wasn't a failure. It was a training session.

CONFIDENCE VS. COURAGE

There's an important distinction I need you to understand: the difference between confidence and courage.

Confidence comes from past success. It's built on evidence. It says, "I've done this before, so I know I can do it again." Confidence is retrospective—it looks backward at what you've accomplished and draws strength from your track record.

Courage comes from future faith. It's built on conviction. It says, "I've never done this before, but I believe God will equip me to do it." Courage is prospective—it looks forward to what you're called to become and steps toward it anyway.

Both are valuable. But only courage can take you to places you've never been.

When I moved to Atlanta the first time, I was operating mostly on courage without the confidence to back it up. When I moved the second time, I had both—the courage of faith plus the confidence of knowing I could build a life in a new place because I was a valuable asset wherever I went.

This is why you have to keep building your courage muscle. Every time you do something scared and survive, you're not just getting through that one challenge. You're creating evidence for yourself. You're building the confidence that will support future acts of courage.

The next leap becomes easier because you remember: Oh yeah, I was scared before, and I made it. God provided before, and He'll provide again.

THE ENTREPRENEURSHIP JOURNEY

Let me give you another example of building courage incrementally.

After we moved to Atlanta, I secured a great position as deputy director of an HR office. Good salary. Good team. Good work. But there was an hour-long commute, and after a while, I was over it.

More than that, though—I knew God was telling me it was time to move into entrepreneurship. Full-time. No more splitting my energy between building someone else's vision and building my own.

But I was afraid.

I didn't come from a line of entrepreneurs. I came from baby boomers who grew up believing that if you get a government job, you've arrived, and you don't quit. Ever.

So even though I knew what God was calling me to do, I hesitated. I took business classes. I got certifications. I joined entrepreneurship groups. I did everything except the thing I was supposed to do: take the leap.

And you know what God did? He made the decision for me.

I took another job—an HR director position a little closer to home. I knew when I accepted it that it wasn't in alignment with what God had called me to. But I convinced myself it was a reasonable compromise. I could build my business on the side, I told myself. I could do both.

But that job didn't give me the autonomy I needed to make the impact I was meant to make. The role was more restrictive than I expected. The environment was more challenging than I anticipated. And I felt God's gentle nudge become a firm push.

Actually, it felt more like a shove. God made me uncomfortable enough to push me into the calling I'd been avoiding.

So in December 2022, after only six months in that position, I quit. I quit a government job. I quit an HR director role. I quit a six-figure salary.

And I launched my business full-time.

THE SPIRITUAL MUSCLE MEMORY

Here's what I want you to understand about that decision: By the time I quit that job in December 2022, I had built the spiritual muscle memory I needed to do it.

I'd moved to Atlanta despite fear. I'd changed jobs multiple times despite other people's questions. I'd followed God's leading even when it didn't make logical sense. And every single time, He had provided. Every single time, things had worked out better than I could have planned.

So when the moment came to make the biggest leap of all —leaving stable employment to become a full-time entrepreneur—I had a track record with God. I had evidence. I had confidence built on past courage.

That's what spiritual muscle memory is: the ability to trust God's plan even when it doesn't make sense to your logical mind, because you've seen Him come through before.

It's like physical muscle memory. A pianist doesn't have to think about where each finger goes once they've practiced enough. A basketball player doesn't have to consciously calculate the angle and force needed for a free throw after shooting thousands of them.

Your body remembers. Your muscles know what to do.

The same thing happens with faith. When you repeatedly choose to trust God, to take action on His calling, to step out even when you're scared—your spirit develops memory. Your faith muscles grow stronger. And eventually, the leap that would have terrified you five years ago becomes the obvious next step.

BUILDING YOUR COURAGE PROTOCOL

So how do you actually build this courage muscle? How do you develop spiritual muscle memory that will sustain you through the leaps you're called to take?

Here's the personalized courage-building protocol I've developed:

Start with micro-moments of courage. You don't build muscle by trying to lift 300 pounds on day one. You start with what you can handle and progressively increase the weight. Same with courage. Take small actions that scare you a little bit. Have the conversation you've been avoiding. Send the email. Make the call. Take the class. Each small act builds the muscle.

Surround yourself with courage-builders. Find people who are where you want to be. Listen to their stories. Join communities of people who are doing scary things. Let their faith feed yours. I stayed grounded by going to church, by listening to sermons that confirmed what God was telling me, by being around people who believed in doing things differently.

Document your wins. Keep a record of the times you did something scared and God came through. Write down the moments when you took action and it worked out. This becomes your evidence file. When fear tries to convince you that you can't do the next thing, you pull out your file and remind yourself: But I did that thing, and that other thing, and that other thing. And God showed up every time.

Reframe failure as training. My failed move to Atlanta in 2006 wasn't a waste. It was preparation. It showed me what I needed to work on, what I needed to develop, what gaps I needed to fill. If you take a leap and it

doesn't go as planned, don't call it failure. Call it a training session for the next attempt.

Pray for courage, not just clarity. We often pray for God to make the path clear before we take the step. But sometimes God wants us to take the step to see the path. Pray for the courage to move even when you can't see the whole journey. Ask for the faith to trust that He'll light the next step when you need it.

Celebrate progress, not just perfection. I didn't move to Atlanta successfully the first time. But I tried. I took action. I was willing to be uncomfortable. That deserves celebration, even though it didn't work out. When you're building courage, you have to honor the attempts, not just the achievements.

THE MOMENTUM EFFECT

Here's what happens when you consistently build your courage muscle: You create unstoppable momentum.

Each act of courage makes the next one easier. Each time you survive doing something scared, you prove to yourself that fear is a liar. Each leap you take expands your sense of what's possible.

And eventually, you become the person who others look at and think, "Wow, they're so brave. I could never do that."

But you know the truth. You're not naturally brave. You just built the muscle. You developed the skill. You trusted the equation: Faith + Action + Community = Unstoppable Momentum.

And now you're living proof that courage isn't about who you are. It's about who you're becoming.

THE INVITATION

So here's what I want you to know: Whatever leap you're being called to take, you can build the courage to do it.

You might not be ready today. You might need to develop the muscle first. You might need to take some smaller steps, surround yourself with the right people, build your evidence file of God's faithfulness.

That's okay. That's not failure. That's training.

But don't confuse "not ready yet" with "never ready." Don't let fear convince you that because you're not strong enough today, you'll never be strong enough.

Start building. Start small if you need to. But start.

Take one micro-moment of courage today. Do one thing that scares you a little bit. Have one conversation you've been avoiding. Take one small action toward the calling you've been circling.

And then do it again tomorrow. And the next day. And the day after that.

Because here's the truth: You're not building courage for its own sake. You're building it because there's a calling on your life that requires it. There's a purpose waiting for you on the other side of fear. There's a version of yourself that you're meant to become, and courage is the bridge that gets you there.

The muscle gets stronger every time you use it. So use it. Build it. Trust the equation.

And watch what happens when faith meets action and community creates unstoppable momentum.

Your leap is waiting. And you're getting stronger every day.

REFLECTION QUESTIONS

1. Think about a time you did something scared and it worked out. What evidence did that experience give you about your ability to handle hard things?
2. On a scale of 1-10, where is your courage muscle right now? What's one micro-moment of courage you could practice this week to build it stronger?
3. Who are the courage-builders in your life? Who needs to be in your community to support the leap you're being called to take?
4. What's the difference between "I'm not ready yet" (which requires training) and "I'm never going to be ready" (which is fear masquerading as wisdom) in your current situation?
5. If you fully trusted the Courage Equation (Faith + Action + Community = Unstoppable Momentum), what would you do differently this week?

SIX

YOUR INNER BOARD OF DIRECTORS

Firing the Voices That Hold You Back

Close your eyes for a second and listen to the conversation happening in your head right now.

Hear it? That committee meeting that's always in session? The one where different voices are weighing in on every decision, every dream, every possibility?

There's the voice that sounds like your mother, reminding you to play it safe. The one that echoes your first boss, telling you to stay in your lane. The old teacher who said you weren't leadership material. The ex who convinced you that you weren't capable of more. The culture that whispers you should be grateful for what you have and stop reaching for more.

We all have this internal board of directors. This collection of voices that influence our decisions, shape our beliefs, and either champion our dreams or kill them before they have a chance to breathe.

Here's the problem: Most of us never consciously chose who gets to sit on our board. We let any random voice take a seat at the table in our minds. And now we're letting people who criticized us twenty years ago cast votes on decisions we're making today.

It's time for a board meeting. And some people are about to get fired.

THE BOARD YOU DIDN'T CHOOSE

Let me tell you about some of the voices that sat on my board for years without my permission.

There was the voice of well-meaning guidance counselors and advisors who told me to make "safe" choices. When I was in undergrad, I had to decide between studying social work or sociology. My heart pulled toward social work—I wanted to help children, serve families, make a direct impact.

But I chose sociology instead. You want to know why? Because I was told that sociology gave me more options. Education was a fallback. It was more "concrete." If the helping profession didn't work out, I could always teach.

It was practical advice. Sensible advice. The kind of guidance that came from people who genuinely wanted me to succeed. But it was also limiting advice. It was advice rooted in fear rather than calling. It was about minimizing risk rather than maximizing purpose.

And I listened to it. Because that's what good students do, right? We listen to the people who know better. We follow the wisdom of those who've gone before us. We make the "smart" choice.

Except here's what nobody tells you: The smart choice for them might be the wrong choice for you.

Then there were the voices of my parents. Baby boomers who stayed at their jobs for decades—my mom for thirty-seven years, my dad for forty-one years. They came up in a time when loyalty meant longevity, when success meant finding a good job and never leaving.

So every time I felt that restlessness, every time I knew it was time to move on from a position, those voices were in my head: "You get a job and you stay. Why are you always leaving? Why can't you just be satisfied?"

They didn't mean to hold me back. They loved me. They wanted security for me. They were passing down the wisdom that had worked for their generation.

But their wisdom was becoming my limitation. Their voices—which had protected me in some seasons—were now preventing me from stepping into my purpose.

THE COMMITTEE IN YOUR HEAD

In corporate settings, we're incredibly intentional about who sits on our actual boards of directors. We vet candidates. We look at their experience, their expertise, their track record. We carefully curate the voices that will guide our organization's future.

But in our minds? We let anyone and everyone have a seat at the table.

The teacher who told you that you weren't good at math still gets to vote on whether you should start that business. The parent who said you should be realistic still gets to weigh in on your dreams. The ex who made you feel small still gets to speak into your self-worth.

And the crazy thing? Some of these people have been gone from your life for years, even decades. But they're still showing up to every meeting, still casting votes, still influencing your decisions.

In my coaching practice, this is one of the most powerful interventions I make with leaders: helping them identify their Internal Advisory Board. Those voices—from parents, teachers, past bosses, society, culture—that influence their decisions without their conscious awareness.

I've seen brilliant executives sabotage their own success because they're still trying to prove themselves to someone who criticized them twenty years ago. I've watched talented professionals turn down opportunities because a voice from their past convinced them they weren't good enough.

Your internal board is running your life whether you acknowledge it or not. The question is: Did you choose these board members intentionally, or did they just show up and take a seat?

FIRING THE VOICES THAT LIMIT YOU

Here's what I've learned from studying organizational behavior and applying it to personal transformation: The voices that helped you survive your past may be the very voices preventing you from stepping into your purpose.

That voice that says "play it safe"? It might have protected you when resources were scarce and risks were genuinely dangerous. But now you're in a different season, and that same voice is keeping you trapped in comfort when God is calling you to courage.

That voice that says "don't draw attention to yourself"? It might have kept you safe in an environment where standing out was risky. But now it's making you invisible when you're meant to be seen.

That voice that says "be grateful for what you have and don't ask for more"? It might have helped your family survive hard times. But now it's blocking your breakthrough.

So how do you fire a board member?

First, you have to identify them. Listen to the voices. Name them. Where did this belief come from? Whose voice is this really? When did I first hear this message?

Second, you thank them for their service. You acknowledge that this voice served a purpose at one time. You honor the protection it provided. You don't have to villainize people who loved you and gave you the best guidance they had.

But third—and this is crucial—you release them from their role. You say, "Thank you, but your term is over. You're no longer serving my vision. You're no longer aligned with where I'm going. Your voice doesn't get a vote anymore."

This doesn't mean you stop loving these people. It doesn't mean you cut off relationships with family or mentors who meant well. It just means you stop letting their limitations become yours.

GET OVER THE NEED TO PLEASE

Let me be direct about something: The need to please will continue to hold you back.

One of the most important things I've had to learn is that the only person I really have to make happy is mc. Me and God need to be on one accord when it comes to what's for me.

That whole idea that you have to please others, that you have to do what's expected of you? I've struggled with that a great deal in my life. I've tried to make people happy. I've tried to do things the way that felt safe because that's what people told me to do.

But here's what I've discovered: When God gives you something, He doesn't necessarily give it to everybody around you.

People may not understand what God has for you because it's going to be different. You were meant to stand out. You weren't meant to fit in and do what everybody else is doing.

As a matter of fact, I literally pray for creative ideas. So if I'm praying for creative ideas but wanting to do things the same way everybody else does, that's a contradiction.

I have to be willing to do things differently and realize that people around me may not understand those things. And that's okay.

The moment you start requiring everyone's understanding and approval before you move is the moment you guarantee you'll stay stuck forever.

SEASONS AND LIFETIMES

Here's another truth you need to understand: Some people are meant to be with you for a season, and some for a lifetime. And everybody is not meant to go with you in every season of life.

If you have people around you who are no longer cheering for you, no longer encouraging you, no longer supporting your dreams, then it may be time to back away.

This doesn't mean you no longer love them. It doesn't mean you don't wish them well. It just means that you're at a different stage in your life, and that's okay.

It also may mean that you have to open yourself up to meeting new people.

Look around. If everybody around you either looks like you, doing what you do, or doing less than you, then you definitely need to broaden your friendship base.

You want people who will stretch you. Now, I don't think friendship should be hard—it definitely should not. But I think in all relationships, both parties should gain.

So what are you gaining and what are you giving when you think about relationships?

If every relationship or every conversation with an individual leaves you depleted, discouraged, like you have to prove your point and fight constantly, then that is probably not the best friendship for you.

If you leave a conversation energized, encouraged, maybe pushed and stretched—because that's what good friends do—then that's a friendship for you.

It's a mutual benefit. It's not just to take and get what you can, but it's about both people growing together.

DIFFERENT PEOPLE FOR DIFFERENT ROLES

Here's something else that's important: Not every person in your life needs to play every role.

Some people are there to encourage you in business. Some are there to encourage you in family matters. Some are there to have fun with. And sometimes, it's just not time to tell everything to everybody.

You always want a mentor—someone who has been there and done that, who can stretch you, who has already driven the road that you're driving so they can give you some encouragement and guidance.

But be clear that your road is still different. The saying goes: Take the meat and throw out the bones.

You cannot mimic every single thing someone else does because you want to make sure that you're true to who you are.

So if someone has an idea or has done something very similar to what you want to do, looking at them and seeing their path is important. But you're not them.

I'm a speaker, and I love speaking all around the world. So there are individuals who speak all around the world, and I can look at them to see what their path was, to see what they did. That's important.

But I'm not them.

YOU SOUND LIKE YOU

For a long time, I struggled with my Southern drawl.

I'm from Virginia, and most people, when I'm talking, will ask where I'm from. For years, I would feel like maybe I didn't know enough vocabulary, or maybe I was a little bit too country, or maybe my dialect wasn't what it should be.

I'd listen to speakers like Tabitha Brown or Brené Brown or Mel Robbins, and I'd think, "Maybe I should sound more like them. Maybe I should have a different delivery style. Maybe my way of speaking isn't professional enough."

But here's what I finally understood: God has called me to do something. So He's given me exactly what I need to do it.

I may not sound just like Tabitha Brown or Brené Brown or Mel Robbins. I sound like Teesha Carter.

And when I don't say what God has placed on my heart to say, when I don't speak in my own voice, then I'm doing those around me a disservice. Because there are people who need to hear my story. There are people who need to hear what I have to say. There are people who need to see me as an example because representation matters.

So I need to ensure that I have people around me who represent where I'm going. People who are mutually benefiting each other. People who understand that we won't do things the exact same way they do because we are uniquely ourselves.

You are uniquely you. And the world needs your voice, not your imitation of someone else's voice.

HIRING YOUR NEW BOARD

So if you're firing the voices that limit you, who are you hiring to replace them?

Here's what your new board should look like:

The Mentor Who's Been There: Someone who's already walked the path you're on. They can share wisdom, warn you about pitfalls, celebrate your wins. But remember: Take the meat, throw out the bones. Learn from their journey without trying to replicate it exactly.

The Encourager: Someone who believes in you even when you're doubting yourself. Who reminds you of who you are when fear tries to convince you of who you're not. Who shows up consistently with energy and encouragement.

The Truth-Teller: Someone who loves you enough to be honest. Who will call you out when you're making excuses. Who will challenge you when you're playing small. Who pushes and stretches you because they see your potential.

The Representation: Someone who looks like where you're going, not where you've been. Someone who's already doing the thing you're trying to do. Someone whose life demonstrates that what you're attempting is possible.

The Faith-Builder: Someone who understands that your purpose is spiritual, not just practical. Who prays with you and for you. Who reminds you that you're not alone in this journey.

These are intentional choices. You don't just wait for the right people to show up. You actively seek them out. You position yourself in spaces where these people gather. You invest in relationships that align with where you're going, not just where you've been.

THE MUTUAL BENEFIT PRINCIPLE

Here's something crucial: Your new board members shouldn't just give to you. You should be giving to them too.

Even in a mentoring relationship, there's mutual benefit. Maybe you're learning from their experience, but they're gaining from your fresh perspective, your energy, your questions that make them think differently.

If a relationship is all take or all give, it's not sustainable. Both parties should be growing. Both should be better because of the connection.

So as you're evaluating who gets to stay on your board and who needs to be released, ask yourself: Is this relationship mutual? Am I learning and growing? Are they learning and growing? Are we both better because we're connected?

If the answer is no, it's time to make a change.

WHEN THE VOICE IS YOUR OWN

Here's the plot twist: Sometimes the voice you need to fire is your own.

That inner critic that tells you you're not good enough? That's not God's voice. That's not truth. That's not wisdom. That's fear wearing a disguise.

That voice that says you should stay small to avoid criticism? That's not protection. That's limitation.

That voice that says who do you think you are to want something bigger? That's not humility. That's false modesty preventing you from stepping into your calling.

You have to learn to distinguish between your voice and God's voice. Between your fear and His calling. Between your limitations and His limitless vision for your life.

God's voice sounds like encouragement. Like calling you higher. Like reminding you that He created you for purpose. Like pushing you toward your potential, not away from it.

Your fear sounds like criticism. Like pulling you lower. Like reminding you of every past failure. Like keeping you trapped in what's familiar rather than launching you toward what's possible.

Learn to recognize the difference. And when you hear fear pretending to be wisdom, fire that voice just like you'd fire any other board member who doesn't serve your vision.

THE BOARD MEETING OF THE MIND

Here's a practical exercise I use with clients: Conduct an actual board meeting of the mind.

Get quiet. Maybe journal. Maybe pray. And ask yourself:

What voices am I currently listening to? Name them specifically.

Where did each voice come from? Who does it sound like?

What message does each voice consistently give me?

Is this message still serving me, or is it limiting me?

If I were to fire this voice, what would I replace it with?

Who do I need to intentionally add to my board?

This isn't a one-time exercise. You should conduct these board meetings regularly. Because as you grow, as seasons change, as your calling evolves, the voices you need will also change.

The mentor who served you perfectly in your twenties might not be the right voice for your forties. The friend who encouraged you in one season might not understand the leap you're being called to take in the next season.

It's okay to make changes. It's okay to thank someone for their service and release them. It's okay to seek out new voices that align with where you're going rather than where you've been.

Your internal board should be as carefully curated as any corporate board. Because the decisions they're guiding aren't just about business—they're about your entire life.

THE INVITATION

So here's my challenge to you: Take inventory of your internal board of directors.

Who's sitting at your table? Whose voices are you listening to? Are they championing your dreams or killing them? Are they speaking life into your calling or death into your potential?

Fire the voices that no longer serve you. Thank them, release them, and let them go.

Hire new advisors who align with where you're headed. Seek out mentors, encouragers, truth-tellers, and faith-builders who will stretch you toward your purpose.

And remember: You sound like you. And that's exactly what the world needs to hear.

Stop trying to mimic someone else's voice, someone else's path, someone else's calling. You are uniquely you, and when you don't speak in your authentic voice, you're doing everyone who needs to hear your message a disservice.

Representation matters. Your story matters. Your voice matters.

Now go conduct that board meeting. Some people are about to get fired. And some new voices are about to change your life.

REFLECTION QUESTIONS

1. Name three specific voices that currently sit on your internal board of directors. Where did each voice come from, and what message does it consistently give you?
2. Which voice has been the most limiting for you? What would change in your life if you fired that voice today?
3. Think about your current relationships. Which ones leave you energized and which ones leave you depleted? What changes do you need to make?
4. Who's missing from your board? What type of person do you need to intentionally seek out to support where you're going?
5. What's one way you've been trying to sound like someone else instead of sounding like yourself? How can you step more fully into your authentic voice?

SEVEN

THE TRANSFORMATION ZONE

What Happens When You Stop Managing and Start Leading

There's a difference between managing your life and leading it.

Management is about maintaining what is. Leadership is about creating what could be.

Management optimizes the status quo. Leadership challenges it.

Management asks, "How do I get better at this?" Leadership asks, "What is God calling me to build?"

And here's what I've learned after two decades in HR, leadership development, and organizational transformation: Most people are managing their lives when they should be leading them. They're maintaining when they should be creating. They're optimizing the wrong thing instead of building the right thing.

The transformation zone—that space where real change happens, where purpose comes alive, where you step into your calling—that's where leaders live. And it's the most uncomfortable, exhilarating, terrifying, beautiful place you'll ever be.

Because transformation doesn't happen in your comfort zone. It happens when you step outside of it.

THE PROFESSOR WHO PUSHED ME

Back in grad school, I had a professor named Dr. Sawyer. And let me tell you—she was tough. Very tough.

At the time, I thought she was just hard on me. I'd turn in work I thought was good, and she'd send it back with notes all over it. She'd challenge my thinking. She'd push me to go deeper, think harder, reach further.

I won't lie—there were moments when I resented it. When I wished I had an easier professor who would just give me the grade and let me move on.

But you know what? After it all, she became my absolute favorite professor. Because she did something that most people won't do: She pushed me. She challenged me. She refused to let me stay comfortable.

She used to say, "You learn best outside your comfort zone."

And I hated hearing it. But she was absolutely right.

Dr. Sawyer was a true gem to me. I still love her and honor all that she taught me to this day. Because she wasn't just teaching me content—she was teaching me how to lead myself. How to expect more from myself. How to step into the transformation zone instead of camping out in the comfort zone.

That's what real leaders do. They take you places you've never been before—including places within yourself that you didn't know existed.

THE TEXT THAT CHANGED THE CONVERSATION

I got a text recently from my cousin. A dear cousin of mine. And it was one of those texts that stops you in your tracks.

"Please help keep me from getting fired today," it said.

I immediately called her. "What's going on?"

"They want me to train a new employee," she said, and I could hear the frustration in her voice. "Training is not on my job description. I don't get paid to train. It is not fair that I have to train someone."

Now, I could have responded with sympathy. I could have agreed that yes, it's frustrating when you're asked to do things outside your official responsibilities. I could have validated her annoyance.

But that would have been managing the situation. And what she needed was leadership.

So here's what I said instead: "Wow, what an excellent honor to be chosen to train. What a resume boost. What an opportunity to excel not only in your performance, but in your training of others."

I kept going: "When opportunities come up for promotion, you'll be considered because they know you can develop others. When you leave that organization and apply for jobs elsewhere, you're no longer just an excellent performer—you're also a trainer. That says lead. That says supervisor. That says manager."

And then I shifted her perspective completely: "Also, consider what you'll be doing for that new employee. You'll be imparting your knowledge. Sharing your skills. Sharing your gifts with that employee. It's an honor."

There was a pause on the other end of the line. And then she said, "Are you always that positive?"

I had to laugh. "You know," I said, "it's just how I think."

COMPENSATION COMES IN MANY FORMS

My mother taught me something that has shaped my entire approach to work and life: "You don't focus on the work. You don't focus on money. You do what you need to do, and you do it at your best, and the money will come."

And I wholeheartedly agree.

But I'd add something to that: Compensation comes in more ways than just money.

When you're truly walking in your purpose, when you're truly living out the design that God has for you and using the gifts that He has blessed you with, grace abounds. Abundance flows to you.

It's important to use your gifts, your calling, to help others. That's what it's all about. It's all about building others up.

But here's what happens when you shift from management thinking to leadership thinking: You stop asking, "What am I getting out of this?" and start asking, "Who am I becoming through this?"

You stop seeing extra responsibilities as burdens and start seeing them as opportunities.

You stop viewing your work through the lens of "is this in my job description?" and start viewing it through the lens of "is this preparing me for where I'm going?"

That's the transformation zone. That's where managers become leaders. That's where maintenance becomes multiplication.

THE OLD LEADERSHIP MODEL

I know that in generations past, leaders operated differently. They hoarded information. They kept knowledge to themselves. They didn't want to share or train because they were afraid.

Why? Because they grew up in a time when you had to hold on to your position. They were fearful that they would be replaced, that someone would do things better than them, that teaching others might threaten their job security.

But that's management thinking. That's scarcity thinking. That's maintaining what you have rather than multiplying what you've been given.

When you operate from that place, you might keep your position, but you'll never expand your impact. You might maintain your authority, but you'll never develop a legacy. You might protect what you have, but you'll never discover what you could become.

THE TRANSFORMATION LEADERSHIP MODEL

Our whole focus as leaders should be to impact others. We should always be focused on sharing, growing, nurturing the next generation.

What are you doing for the next generation? Are you using what God has given you—your gifts, your talents, your experience—to bless others?

That's what I do. I do this every day. I build leaders.

My whole purpose here is to leave a legacy. A legacy of discipleship, where I show first God, then family, and then work. Where I demonstrate that it's possible to live in your purpose and thrive.

It's important that everybody I touch, everybody I impact, is left better than when I first met them.

That's transformational leadership. And it requires a completely different mindset than management.

Management asks: "How do I protect what I have?"

Leadership asks: "How do I multiply what I've been given?"

Management says: "Don't train them too well or they'll replace you."

Leadership says: "Train them so well they could replace you, then keep growing so you're ready for the next level."

Management focuses on tasks.

Leadership focuses on transformation.

THE SWIMMING LESSONS THAT TAUGHT ME ABOUT LEADERSHIP

Let me tell you about the time I had to lead myself into one of the most uncomfortable situations I'd ever voluntarily entered.

I've been terrified of swimming my entire life. Not just uncomfortable—terrified. The kind of fear that made me turn down vacation activities, miss out on experiences with friends, feel embarrassed at pool parties while everyone else was in the water having fun.

For years, I told myself it was fine. I had my reasons. I'd work around it. I'd just stay on the beach while everyone else enjoyed the water. No big deal.

Except it was a big deal. Because that fear was limiting my life in ways I didn't want to admit.

Meanwhile, I made absolutely sure both my boys learned to swim when they were young. I wasn't going to let my fear become their limitation. They swim like fish now. I wasn't going to let my baggage become theirs.

But what about my life? What about my limitations?

In 2023, at over forty years old, I made a decision. I signed up for swimming lessons. Not group lessons where I could hide in the back and blend in with other adults who were "just brushing up on their technique." Private lessons. One-on-one. Just me and an instructor, with nowhere to hide and no way to pretend I was anything other than a complete beginner.

I'd actually tried group lessons before, years earlier. But this time was different. This time I had a catalyst: I had a trip to Aruba coming up, and I was tired. Tired of sitting on the beach. Tired of watching everyone else participate in water activities. Tired of letting fear masquerade as "being realistic" or "knowing my limits."

I was done managing my fear. I was ready to lead myself through it.

SHOWING UP AS A BEGINNER

Let me tell you, showing up to those first lessons was humbling in a way I hadn't anticipated.

The facility had classes running throughout the day, and most of the people I'd see before and after my session? Little kids. Children learning to swim at the age when you're supposed to learn. Five-year-olds. Seven-year-olds. Kids who didn't think twice about looking silly or making mistakes because that's what learning looks like.

And there I was. A professional speaker. A successful entrepreneur. A woman with two grown sons and decades of life experience. Standing on the side of the pool in my swimsuit, about to admit to a stranger that I couldn't do something most people learn in elementary school.

Every part of me wanted to make excuses. To explain my whole history with water. To justify why I'd waited this long. To somehow demonstrate that I was competent and accomplished in other areas even though I was completely incompetent at this one thing.

But my instructor didn't need my life story. She needed me to get in the water.

So I did.

And you know what I learned in those first few lessons? The same lesson Dr. Sawyer taught me in grad school, the same lesson that applies to every transformation I've ever guided someone through:

You learn best outside your comfort zone.

Not near your comfort zone. Not adjacent to it. Outside of it. In the place where you feel vulnerable and exposed and like you might fail at any moment.

That's where transformation lives.

THE CHOICE TO FOCUS

Here's what I had to do during those swimming lessons: I had to make a conscious choice about where to put my focus.

I could focus on the embarrassment. On the fact that children half my age were doing this better than me. On the possibility that I might look foolish. On all the years I'd wasted by not learning this earlier.

Or I could focus on my mission. On what I was becoming. On the freedom I was creating for myself. On the experiences that were waiting for me on the other side of this discomfort.

Every single lesson, I had to make that choice again. Focus on the discomfort, or focus on the transformation.

This is what leadership looks like, by the way. Not just in swimming pools, but in every area of life where you're trying to grow. Leadership isn't about never feeling uncomfortable. It's about consciously choosing where you direct your attention when discomfort shows up.

Managers try to eliminate discomfort. Leaders move through it with intention.

I couldn't let those invisible handcuffs—embarrassment, pride, the fear of looking like a beginner—keep me from experiencing what I knew I was capable of becoming.

WHAT I GAINED

By the end of my time with that instructor, I could float. My breathing still wasn't perfect—honestly, it's still not. I don't swim like Michael Phelps. I'm not going to compete in triathlons.

But I can get from one side of the pool to the other. I can back-paddle. I can participate in water activities that I couldn't before.

And when I went to Aruba? Everything was different.

Not because the destination changed—I'd been to Aruba before. But because I showed up different. More confident. More capable. More free.

I participated in experiences I never could have before. I wasn't sitting on the beach watching everyone else have fun. I was in the water. I was present. I was living fully instead of partially.

That trip felt different because I had led myself through discomfort and come out transformed on the other side.

THE LEADERSHIP LESSON

Here's what those swimming lessons taught me about leadership—the kind of leadership that transforms your life:

Leaders go first into uncomfortable places. Nobody forced me to take those lessons. Nobody required me to face that fear. I had to lead myself there. That's what leaders do—they go first, even when it's scary.

Leaders embrace being beginners. I had to be willing to look foolish, to make mistakes, to be incompetent in

front of someone else. That's humility. That's the prerequisite for growth. You can't become good at something new without first being bad at it.

Leaders focus on mission over minor inconveniences. Yes, it was embarrassing. Yes, it was uncomfortable. But those were minor inconveniences compared to what I was gaining—freedom, capability, new experiences, the ability to participate fully in my own life.

Leaders set an example, whether they intend to or not. My sons already knew how to swim, but they watched their mother face a decades-old fear and do something about it. That's a different kind of lesson. That's showing them that growth doesn't have an age limit. That it's never too late to become who you're meant to be.

Leaders don't let past limitations define future possibilities. I'd spent forty-plus years not swimming. That was history. But it didn't have to be my destiny. The story could change at any moment I chose to rewrite it.

This is the transformation zone. This is what happens when you stop managing your limitations and start leading yourself through them.

You don't overcome fear by eliminating it. You overcome it by doing the thing anyway. By showing up as a beginner. By focusing on what you're becoming instead of what you're leaving behind. By choosing, again and again, to let transformation matter more than comfort.

Dr. Sawyer was right all those years ago. You learn best outside your comfort zone. Transformation happens most outside of your comfort zone.

So take the step. Do the thing. Sign up for the lessons—literal or metaphorical—that will expand who you are and what you're capable of.

You know what it is. It just seems impossible. It seems too hard. It seems too late. You're too old, too established, too far along to start something new.

But you're not. Those are just the thoughts that keep you managing instead of leading. Those are just the lies that keep you comfortable instead of transformed.

In the words of Oprah Winfrey: "I control the thermostat."

You control the thermostat too. You set the temperature. You determine the atmosphere. You choose whether you're going to let comfort dictate your choices or let calling lead the way.

FROM MANAGEMENT TO LEADERSHIP IN YOUR OWN LIFE

So what does this look like when you stop managing your life and start leading it?

It means you stop asking, "How do I get better at maintaining this comfortable existence?" and start asking, "What is God calling me to build that doesn't exist yet?"

It means you stop optimizing your current reality and start creating a new one.

It means you stop viewing challenges as problems to avoid and start seeing them as the very thing that will transform you into who you're meant to become.

Let me be specific about what this shift looks like:

Management mindset: "I need to protect my position."

Leadership mindset: "I need to prepare others so well that I'm ready for my next assignment."

Management mindset: "Extra responsibilities are a burden."

Leadership mindset: "Extra responsibilities are preparation for where I'm going."

Management mindset: "I should be compensated fairly for my work."

Leadership mindset: "I'm being compensated in ways I can't even see yet—in skills, relationships, character development, and divine positioning."

Management mindset: "I'll step up when I feel ready."

Leadership mindset: "I'll step up because that's how I become ready."

Management mindset: "I need comfort to thrive."

Leadership mindset: "I need challenge to grow."

See the difference? Same circumstances, completely different approach.

THE SPIRITUAL SHIFT

In Scripture, God doesn't call us to manage our talents. He calls us to multiply them.

Remember the parable? The servants who were given different amounts of money? The ones who invested, who took risks, who multiplied what they were given—they were praised. The one who buried his talent in the ground to keep it safe? He was rebuked.

God isn't impressed by maintenance. He's looking for multiplication.

When you embrace your role as a leader—even if you're only leading yourself at first—you start making decisions based on vision rather than fear. On calling rather than comfort. On multiplication rather than maintenance.

You stop asking, "What's the safest choice?" and start asking, "What's the most faithful choice?"

You stop worrying about protecting what you have and start focusing on becoming who you're called to be.

That's the spiritual shift from management to leadership. And it changes everything.

LEADERSHIP PRINCIPLES FOR YOUR TRANSFORMATION

Let me share some fundamental leadership principles I've used with Fortune 500 executives, and show you how to apply them to your own transformation journey:

1. Leaders Go First

You can't wait for someone else to show you how it's done. You can't wait for permission or perfect conditions. Leaders step out first. They model what's possible. They go to uncomfortable places so others can follow.

2. Leaders Develop Others

Even if you don't have a team, you're developing someone. Your children. Your community. The people who are watching you. Leaders understand that their transformation gives others permission to transform too.

3. Leaders Make Decisions With Incomplete Information

Managers wait for perfect clarity. Leaders move on conviction. You'll never have all the information you want, but you can have all the faith you need.

4. Leaders Accept Discomfort as Part of Growth

If you're comfortable all the time, you're not leading—you're maintaining. Leaders expect to be uncomfortable. They know that's where transformation lives.

5. Leaders Focus on What's Being Built, Not Just What's Being Done

Managers complete tasks. Leaders build legacies. Every action you take is either maintaining what is or creating what could be. Choose creation.

YOU ARE THE CEO OF YOUR OWN TRANSFORMATION

Here's what I need you to understand: You are the CEO of your own life. Not the manager. The CEO.

That means you're responsible for the vision, not just the execution. You're accountable for where you're going, not just where you are. You're in charge of transformation, not just maintenance.

And that requires you to show up differently. To think differently. To see opportunities where others see obligations. To see preparation where others see problems. To see purpose where others see paychecks.

When you're the CEO of your transformation, you stop waiting for someone else to promote you into your purpose. You promote yourself. You give yourself permission. You step into the role you're called to play.

The world is waiting for what you have to offer. But you can't offer it while you're still in management mode. You have to step into leadership.

THE INVITATION

So here's my challenge to you: Stop managing. Start leading.

Stop maintaining what is. Start creating what could be.

Stop optimizing for comfort. Start optimizing for calling.

Stop asking, "What's in it for me?" Start asking, "Who am I becoming through this?"

Transformation doesn't happen in the comfort zone. It happens when you say yes to the mission trip that terrifies you. When you say yes to training the new employee even though it's not in your job description. When you say yes to the calling that doesn't make sense to anyone else but makes perfect sense to you and God.

You learn best outside your comfort zone. Dr. Sawyer was right.

So step outside. Do the thing. Lead yourself into the transformation zone.

Because the world doesn't need more people managing their lives. The world needs people leading the way into what's possible.

And you're exactly the leader we've been waiting for.

REFLECTION QUESTIONS

1. In what areas of your life are you managing (maintaining) rather than leading (creating)? Be specific.

2. Think about a recent opportunity that felt like a burden. How would viewing it through a leadership lens change your perspective?

3. What's one uncomfortable thing you could say yes to this week that would stretch you into the transformation zone?

4. If you truly saw yourself as the CEO of your own transformation, what decision would you make differently today?

5. Who's watching you? What example are you setting for the next generation through how you approach challenges and opportunities?

EIGHT

BUILDING YOUR LAUNCH PAD

Creating the Systems That Support Your Leap

You can't just jump and hope for the best.

I know we've been talking a lot about faith, about taking leaps, about doing things scared. And all of that is true and necessary. But here's what's also true: Faith without works is dead. And works without systems is chaos.

You need both. You need the courage to take the leap and the infrastructure to sustain it.

Think about it this way: NASA doesn't just put astronauts in a rocket and light a match. There's a launch pad. There's a system. There's preparation, testing, backup plans, support structures. All of that makes the actual launch possible.

Your leap needs a launch pad too. And in this chapter, I'm going to show you exactly how to build it.

THE FOUNDATION OF EVERYTHING

Before anything else—before the vision boards, before the planning, before the practical systems—comes prayer.

I know I've said this before, but it bears repeating: You have to pray and nurture your relationship with God.

Nurturing your relationship with God means praying before doing something. It means ensuring that you're in alignment with what He has for you. It means reading the

Bible, studying Scripture, communing with like-minded people, attending worship.

God uses different people, different forms to communicate with you. And so before I move on anything significant, I'm clear that this is what God has for me.

Prayer isn't just something you do once and check off the list. It's the ongoing conversation that keeps you grounded, aligned, and connected to the source of your calling.

This is your spiritual infrastructure. Everything else you build rests on this foundation.

Without it, you might have a impressive structure, but it won't withstand the storms. With it, you can weather anything that comes your way.

WRITE THE VISION AND MAKE IT PLAIN

Once you're grounded in prayer, the next step is to write it out.

There's a verse in Habakkuk that says, "Write the vision and make it plain." That's not just good spiritual advice—it's good practical advice.

For me, this takes two forms: vision boards and lists.

Vision boards are like pre-planning. They help you get clear on what you're building, where you're going, what your life is supposed to look like when you're living in your purpose. They keep the destination visible when the journey gets hard.

But then you need lists. Practical, detailed lists of what you need to actually do to make that vision a reality.

I'm a very organized person, and I use lists religiously. And I'll tell you why: it gives me gratification to cross something off the list. To see that something is actually being done. To track progress in a tangible way.

Lists turn vision into action. They take the dream from abstract to concrete. They give you the next step when you're not sure what to do.

So write it out. Both the big picture and the small steps. Both the vision and the to-do list. You need both to build a successful launch pad.

PLAN YOUR DAY

Here's something I've learned the hard way: If it's not on my calendar, it doesn't exist.

I use my iPhone calendar like it's my life support system. Because in a very real way, it is. It's how I ensure that the things that matter actually happen.

You need to plan your day. Use your planner—electronic or paper, it doesn't matter. But use something.

Plan appointments. Plan time to actually do things that need to be done. If it's something you do every week or every month, put it on your calendar.

For example, I have a money day. Once a month, I sit down and do my mileage, reconcile my receipts, make sure everything is organized for taxes. I don't wait until the end of the year when it's overwhelming. I handle it monthly because it's on my calendar.

Anything that's needed to make sure you're moving in the right direction, you want to add it to your calendar.

If you're studying, going to school, taking a class—make sure you plan time to work on that. If you're building a business on the side while working full-time, block out the hours you'll dedicate to it.

For me, I'm a morning person, so I would do my most important work in the morning before my kids woke up. Some people do it in the evening once kids go to bed. Some people do it at lunchtime.

But here's the key: Put it on your calendar. Because your calendar is an accountability tool. When something is scheduled, you're far more likely to actually do it than when it's just floating around in your mind as something you "should" get to eventually.

FEED YOUR MIND

Read as much as you can. Whether that's audio books, physical books, online courses, or taking classes—make sure you're constantly fueling your mind.

And be intentional about what you're learning. You want to be constantly learning in the direction you want to go.

If it's something in finance, make sure you're feeding your mind with that. If it's human resources, make sure you're feeding your mind with that. Medical field, entrepreneurship, leadership—whatever your goals are, continue to surround yourself with information and knowledge in that area.

This isn't optional. This is infrastructure.

Your mind is the engine that drives everything else. If you're not maintaining it, upgrading it, fueling it with the right inputs, eventually it's going to break down.

So make learning a system, not a luxury. Schedule it. Budget for it. Prioritize it.

SELF-CARE IS NOT SELFISH

I cannot say this enough: You cannot pour from an empty cup.

If you're already depleted, it's very hard to get to where you're going. Self-care isn't selfish—it's strategic. It's infrastructure. It's necessary maintenance for the vehicle that's going to carry you to your purpose.

For me, self-care looks like several things:

Vacations: I take a vacation four times a year. One time with family. One time on a girls' trip. One time with my husband. And it used to be one time with my mom before she passed, so now that's with my sister or my best friend or something like that.

But the point is: I plan rest. I schedule joy. I make sure I'm refilling my cup regularly, not just when I'm completely empty and falling apart.

Small Luxuries: I also enjoy having my nails done. So what I'll do is actually go get my nails painted before I have to speak or before I have an engagement, because that makes me feel good. That makes me feel like my cup is full. It gives me the confidence I need to move forward.

Find what fills your cup. Maybe it's not nails—maybe it's a massage, a long walk in nature, coffee with a friend, a weekend away, time to read a novel. Whatever it is, make it part of your system.

Remove the Distractions: Self-care also means protecting your peace. There are going to be haters. There are going to be people who don't understand what you're doing. People who don't celebrate what you're doing.

But you want to limit your exposure to that as much as possible.

If that means limiting your circle, that may be what you have to do. It doesn't mean you don't care about the people. It doesn't mean that you don't love them. It just means that in this season, that's not healthy for where you're trying to go.

If you're doing any activities that take away or remove you from your goals, pray and ask God to give you what you need to remove those things. To give you the strength to create boundaries. To help you protect the vision He's given you.

MOVE YOUR BODY

Exercise. I know, I know—it sounds cliché. But it is very important to take care of your physical body.

Your body and your mind work together. You can't neglect one and expect the other to perform at its peak.

For me, I walk. I love walking. I just recently started Pilates. I also like hiking. But whatever you like to do, find it and do it.

I can't tell you a specific exercise to do. Yoga is good. Running is good. Swimming is good. Weight training is good. The point isn't which exercise you choose—it's that you move.

Build movement into your system. Put it on your calendar. Make it non-negotiable.

Because when the stress of your leap gets intense—and it will—your body needs to be strong enough to handle it.

FUEL YOUR BODY

I'm a pescatarian. Not everyone is going to be a pescatarian, and I'm not saying you have to be. But I am saying you want to make sure you're fueling your body properly.

Your body and your mind work together. So you want to fuel your mind and your body with healthy foods, healthy images, healthy things to help you reach those goals that you have.

Think about it: If you're feeding your body junk food, you're going to feel sluggish. If you're feeding your mind junk content, you're going to think small. If you're feeding your spirit junk relationships, you're going to stay stuck.

What you consume matters. In every area.

So be intentional about what you're putting in. Your launch pad needs to be built with quality materials, not whatever happens to be convenient in the moment.

GET THE CREDENTIALS YOU NEED

If there is a certification, degree, or some type of education you need to reach your goals, take the steps to get it as soon as possible.

Putting it off and procrastinating pushes you further and further away from your dreams and goals. And honestly, it actually makes you depleted and takes your confidence down.

So just knock it out. Instead of procrastinating about it, really put a plan in place. Put it on your calendar. Make a deadline and get it done.

Even if you have to do it again, don't give up. Make sure you get the credentialing that you need so that won't be a hindrance from helping you reach your goals.

I see this happen too often: People know what they need to do. They know what credential or certification would open doors. But they wait. They tell themselves, "I'll do it next year." Or "I'll wait until I have more time."

But next year comes and they still haven't done it. And the extra time never materializes.

Meanwhile, opportunities pass them by because they don't have the credentials to qualify.

Don't let that be you. If you know you need something, build a plan to get it. Now. Not someday. Now.

THE LAUNCH PAD STRATEGY

Let me pull all of this together into what I call the Launch Pad Strategy.

This is a carefully constructed foundation that supports your leap. It's not just about taking action—it's about taking strategic action. It's about building infrastructure that can sustain you through the transition.

Here's what your launch pad needs:

1. Spiritual Foundation

Prayer, Scripture, worship, community. This is non-negotiable. Without this, everything else will eventually crumble.

2. Clear Vision

Vision boards and written goals. You need to know where you're going. "I want something different" isn't a vision—it's a feeling. Get specific.

3. Daily Systems

Calendar management, task lists, routines that ensure important things actually happen. Systems eliminate the need for constant decision-making and willpower.

4. Financial Planning

Budget for your transition. Build emergency funds. Create multiple income streams if possible. Money stress can kill momentum, so address it proactively.

5. Physical and Mental Health

Exercise, nutrition, rest, self-care. Your body is the vehicle carrying you to your purpose. Maintain it.

6. Continuous Learning

Books, courses, mentors, classes. Keep feeding your mind in the direction you're going.

7. Credential Acquisition

Get the degrees, certifications, licenses you need. Don't let lack of credentials be the reason you can't pursue what you're called to.

8. Community and Relationships

Build your network before you need it. Surround yourself with people who support your vision. Limit exposure to those who drain you.

9. Boundary Protection

Learn to say no to things that don't serve your vision. Protect your peace. Guard your time and energy.

When you have all of these elements in place, you're not just jumping and hoping for the best. You're launching from a stable platform that can handle the G-forces of transformation.

BUILD YOUR NETWORK BEFORE YOU NEED IT

One of the biggest mistakes I see people make is waiting until they need help to start building relationships.

They quit their job before they've made any connections in their new industry. They launch their business before they've built a support network. They take the leap without having built the net.

But here's what smart leaders do: They build their network before they need it.

When I was working full-time, I was already attending entrepreneurship groups. I was already connecting with other business owners. I was already learning from people who were doing what I wanted to do.

So when I finally took the leap into full-time entrepreneurship, I wasn't starting from scratch. I had relationships. I had resources. I had people I could call.

Start now. Join the groups. Attend the conferences. Connect with people on LinkedIn. Have coffee with someone who's doing what you want to do.

Your network is part of your launch pad. Build it intentionally.

CREATE MULTIPLE INCOME STREAMS

If possible, start creating additional income streams before you leave your primary source of income.

This doesn't mean you have to have everything figured out. But it does mean you should be building something on the side if you know you're eventually going to make a transition.

When I was working my HR director job, I was already taking on consulting projects. I was already speaking at events. I was already building my reputation and my client base.

So when I finally left full-time employment, I wasn't starting at zero. I had momentum. I had proof of concept. I had income already flowing, even if it wasn't enough to fully support me yet.

This is strategic. This is infrastructure. This is building your launch pad.

ESTABLISH DAILY PRACTICES

Your launch pad also includes the daily practices that keep you grounded when everything else is shifting.

For me, that includes:

Morning prayer and devotional time

Planning my day every morning

Moving my body

Checking in with my husband about our schedules

Reviewing my goals weekly

Protecting time for learning

These practices might seem small, but they're the scaffolding that holds everything else up when things get turbulent.

When you take a big leap, there will be days when you doubt yourself. Days when you wonder if you made the right choice. Days when the old comfortable life looks really appealing.

On those days, your daily practices will carry you through. They'll keep you moving forward even when motivation is low. They'll remind you why you leaped in the first place.

Don't underestimate the power of daily practices. They're not just habits—they're infrastructure.

TURNING YOUR LEAP INTO A LAUNCH

Here's the difference between a leap and a launch:

A leap is impulsive, reactive, hoping for the best. A launch is intentional, strategic, prepared for multiple scenarios.

A leap says, "I'm out of here!" A launch says, "I've built the infrastructure to support this transition, and now I'm ready to go."

A leap depends on luck. A launch depends on systems.

Both require courage. Both require faith. But a launch also requires planning.

That's what this chapter has been about. Turning your leap of faith into a strategic launch by building the systems, relationships, resources, and routines that will support you when things get hard.

Because they will get hard. There will be turbulence. There will be moments when you wonder if you're going to make it.

And on those days, your launch pad will be what holds you steady. Your systems will be what keep you moving forward. Your infrastructure will be what prevents you from falling back into the comfortable prison you just escaped.

THE INVITATION

So here's what I want you to do: Start building your launch pad today.

Don't wait until you're ready to leap. Don't wait until you've made the decision. Start building now.

Put systems in place. Schedule your self-care. Join the groups. Make the connections. Get the credentials. Establish the routines.

Because when the moment comes—when God makes it clear that it's time to move—you want to be ready. You want to have a platform that can support your leap.

Faith without works is dead. But works without systems is chaos.

Build the infrastructure. Create the systems. Construct your launch pad.

And then, when it's time, you won't just be taking a leap of faith. You'll be launching into your purpose with everything you need to sustain the journey.

Your purpose is waiting. Your calling is ready. Your launch pad is being built.

The only question is: What are you going to add to it today?

REFLECTION QUESTIONS

1. Which element of your launch pad is strongest right now? Which element is weakest or missing entirely?
2. What's one system you could put in place this week that would support your eventual leap? (Schedule it now.)
3. Look at your calendar. Does it reflect your priorities and your calling, or does it reflect everyone else's demands on your time?
4. Who's already in your network that could support your transition? Who do you need to intentionally connect with?
5. What credential, certification, or education do you need? What's your plan and timeline to get it? (Be specific—vague plans don't get executed.)

NINE

THE RIPPLE EFFECT

How Your Leap Gives Others Permission to Fly

Your life is bigger than your own.

I know that sounds paradoxical. How can your life be bigger than your own? But here's what I mean: When you take that leap, when you step into your purpose, when you follow God's calling even when it's scary, you're not just changing your life. You're changing the lives of everyone who's watching.

And trust me, people are watching. Even when you think no one notices. Even when you feel alone in your journey. Even when it seems like nobody understands what you're doing.

Someone is watching. Someone is waiting. Someone is silently praying that if you can do it, maybe they can too.

Your transformation isn't just about you. It's about the ripple effect. It's about how your courage becomes permission for someone else's leap. It's about how your faith becomes a catalyst for someone else's breakthrough.

We are the hands and feet of Jesus. And Jesus uses our experiences, both the triumphs and the trials, to bless, encourage, and motivate others.

THE COVENANT THAT CHANGED EVERYTHING

Let me tell you about my marriage.

My husband and I have been married for, well, by the time you're reading this, it'll be twenty years. I got married at twenty-seven, which is kind of young by 2025 standards. And staying married for twenty years? That's becoming less and less common.

Usually when I tell people, they're like, "Oh, that's been a long time."

And here's what's interesting: Very early on, my husband and I realized that we had a covenant. Not just a marriage of convenience. Not just financial partnership. Not just love. But literally a covenant between him, me, and God.

It was bigger than us.

We got married for us, of course. We got married for our children. But we also got married for the countless people who are watching. Who need an example. Who need a relatable example. Who need an example that looks like them, that has similar challenges and similar triumphs, that lives their everyday life.

And yet through happy times and sad times, through trials and tribulations, we still make it.

That's not because we're perfect. That's not because marriage is easy for us. That's because we understand that our marriage is part of something bigger than our feelings on any given day.

People need to see that it's possible. That you can build a life with someone and sustain it. That covenant isn't just an old-fashioned word. It's a powerful commitment that carries you through seasons when feelings alone wouldn't be enough.

THE LEAP THAT INSPIRED OTHERS

When I took that leap in 2023, when I quit my government job in December of 2022 and went full-time into entrepreneurship, I had no idea how many people were watching.

I was focused on my own fear, my own doubts, my own questions about whether I was making the right choice. I was thinking about my family, my finances, my future.

What I wasn't thinking about was the ripple effect.

But here's what started happening: People began coming to me and telling me that I was an inspiration. That because of me, they'd been willing to take a leap. That they'd been watching what I was building and it gave them the courage to believe they could build something too.

Especially on those days when it gets a little rough, when entrepreneurship feels hard, when the income is unpredictable, when I wonder if I made the right choice, hearing someone say "you inspire me" is powerful.

Because here's what I've learned: People you don't even realize are looking at what you're doing, what you're building. And many times, it gives them the hope that they need.

Your struggle isn't just your struggle. Your breakthrough isn't just your breakthrough. Your transformation isn't just about you getting to a better place. It's about showing others what's possible.

THE COST OF BEING FIRST

I tell people all the time: It's difficult to be the change in a family. It's difficult to be the first in a family.

You have to work hard. Sometimes you have to go against what's the norm. Sometimes you have to go against even those who may not believe in you. But you have to stay true to your calling.

When you do that, when you break the patterns, when you challenge the limitations, when you step into something nobody in your family has done before, it inspires others.

Sometimes it doesn't. And those people who don't get on the bandwagon, those people who continue to hate or not support or not encourage you? You pray for them and leave them where they are.

But for those who need that example, for those who need that push, for those who need to see in real life someone doing it while juggling marriage and family and responsibility? Your life becomes their permission slip.

You're not just living your life. You're showing others what's possible in theirs.

THE GIFT OF TIME

Let me tell you about one of the most profound ripple effects of my leap into entrepreneurship: the time I got to spend with my mother before she passed.

I lost my mom in October of 2023. And I'm a believer that things aren't by chance. I think that God turns things around for bad and uses them for good.

Because of the fact that I had gone into full-time entrepreneurship in 2023, I had spent so much time with my mother that year.

She still lived in Virginia. I was living in Atlanta. But either I was in Virginia with her, or she was with me in Atlanta, or we were traveling somewhere together.

That year, we went to Orlando, Florida. For many years, she had said she wanted to go to Orlando. So we got to have that experience together. She went with me to a conference.

We went to Aruba. She and my bonus dad and my husband and I experienced Aruba together. It was amazing.

I was home for weeks and weeks and weeks at a time because much of what I do now, I can do virtually. I don't have to be at a desk in a specific location.

We'd always talked all day, every day. But that dedicated time we could spend together? That was a gift.

And so even through the trial of losing her, I was able to be home while she was in the hospital. She was there for one week, and my dad and my sister and I took turns. We didn't leave her alone that whole time.

I was able to do that. And then after, I was able to stay home in Virginia for a couple of months just to ensure things were set up, to be there for my family, to grieve without having to worry about whether I'd used up all my bereavement leave or whether I had enough PTO.

When I went back to work, I was able to do that virtually because I had started my business.

And so that gives people hope. Hope in the flexibility that entrepreneurship gave me. The hope and honestly, the security that it gave me. I didn't have to worry about whether I had enough leave. I was able to do it because I had a flexible career.

Entrepreneurship gave me that flexibility.

When people have many different things they have to juggle, family crises, aging parents, unexpected challenges, seeing someone navigate that while still building a business gives them hope. It shows them that there are options. That there are ways to design a life that can hold both purpose and presence.

THE GRIND THAT INSPIRES

Here's another example of the ripple effect: When I was working on my master's thesis, I had a newborn baby. I had just gotten married. I had a six-year-old. I worked full-time. And my college was a commute, probably about thirty to forty-five minutes away.

So I had to go to school in Norfolk or Portsmouth for my classes. And I was juggling all of that. New marriage. New baby. Older child. Full-time career. Graduate school.

When people see that grind, when people see that you're able to juggle and come out on top, that inspires and encourages them.

I didn't do it to inspire anyone. I was just trying to survive, to get through, to accomplish what I knew I was supposed to accomplish.

But looking back, I can see how many people were watching. How many people saw a young mother pursuing education while building a family and maintaining a career, and thought, "Maybe I can do that too."

That's the ripple effect. You may not even realize you're creating it, but you are.

REFRAMING THE QUESTION

So instead of asking, like many people do, "Why me? Why did this have to happen to me? Why do I have to face this challenge? Why is this so hard?"

Instead of that, see it as God using you to bless someone else.

Your struggle has a purpose beyond your own growth. Your challenge has a meaning beyond your own character development. Your journey has an impact beyond your own transformation.

It's a ripple effect. You may be the change, you may be number one, you may be the first. But look at how many people would benefit from some of the experiences that you've had.

Look at how many people need to see that it's possible. That you can be a young mother and still pursue education. That you can lose a parent and still build a business. That you can take a risk and not just survive but thrive.

You're not going through it just for you. You're going through it for everyone who's watching, wondering if they can make it too.

INDIVIDUAL TRANSFORMATION IS NEVER INDIVIDUAL

Here's one of the most profound discoveries from my coaching practice: Individual transformation is never really individual.

When one person in a family system, team, or organization steps into their authentic power, it shifts the entire dynamic.

I've watched marriages improve when one spouse pursued their calling. I've seen teams become more innovative when their leader embraced vulnerability. I've witnessed organizations transform when key players stopped playing small.

Your leap doesn't just change your life. It changes the lives of everyone watching.

Think about it: When you stop settling for mediocrity, the people around you start questioning their own settling. When you start prioritizing your purpose, the people around you start examining their own priorities. When you demonstrate courage, you give others permission to be brave.

You're creating a ripple effect whether you intend to or not. The question is: What kind of ripples are you creating?

THE SCIENCE OF SOCIAL CONTAGION

There's actual science behind this. Research shows that behaviors, attitudes, and even emotions are contagious within social networks.

If you start exercising, people in your network are more likely to start exercising. If you go back to school, people around you are more likely to pursue education. If you take a career risk, people you know become more willing to take their own risks.

This isn't just inspiration. This is social contagion. It's how change spreads through communities, through families, through organizations.

You're not just living your life. You're modeling what's possible. You're expanding what people believe is achievable. You're rewriting the collective story about what people like you can do.

That's powerful. That's impact. That's the ripple effect.

THE SPIRITUALITY OF INFLUENCE

In Scripture, we're called to be light in dark places. We're called to be salt that adds flavor. We're called to be cities on hills that can't be hidden.

Sometimes that means being the first person to show others what's possible.

You don't need a title to be influential. You don't need a platform to be a leader. You don't need permission to start modeling the transformation you want to see in your community.

You just need to be willing to go first. To try first. To risk first. To believe first.

And then watch what happens when others see you and think, "If they can do it, maybe I can too."

That's the spirituality of influence. That's being the hands and feet of Jesus. That's using your experiences, both positive and negative, to bless, encourage, and motivate others.

STORIES OF THE RIPPLE EFFECT

Let me share some specific examples of ripple effects I've witnessed:

There was a young lady who really enjoyed cooking. She'd cooked with her grandmother, which was a beautiful experience. Her grandmother had since passed, and she really wanted to cook professionally, but she couldn't see her way. She didn't know how to start. She had no formal training. She needed financing.

We worked together on an action plan, and she started her business. She started with cooking dinners for special events, for couples. Then she narrowed it down to desserts. She realized that's really where her passion lay.

She had to try some things and take the first step to narrow down and niche down to exactly what God was calling her to do. Now she sells at vendor fairs, fall festivals, schools. She sells by word of mouth. And it's going to continue to grow because she took the leap.

But here's the thing: Her courage is now inspiring her son, her siblings, her community. They're watching a woman who looked at her circumstances, decided they didn't define her future, and built something beautiful.

Another example: I had a young lady who wanted to start a t-shirt business. She initially came to me thinking that t-shirts were too saturated, everybody sells t-shirts. But I assured her that when you're doing something from the heart, God makes room. He makes room for our gifts. He makes room for our talents. And there's enough for everybody.

She started an online business where she sells t-shirts with inspirational messages. And they're booming. She gets gratification when someone who she doesn't know buys the t-shirts. Now it's expanded to other items, personal items, phone covers, laptop covers, but they're all inspirational.

The whole intention is that when you look at these things, you're inspired. So she's using her gift, her talent, to inspire and encourage others.

And now? Other people in her network are starting their own businesses. They're thinking, "If she can do it, so can I."

That's the ripple effect.

FROM EMPLOYEE TO STATE REPRESENTATIVE

Here's another powerful example: There was one young lady who was working with me at one point, and she really wanted to be an attorney.

I always tell employees: I'm here to help you grow, whether it's in this organization or outside of this organization. So I helped coach her in leadership. I helped train her in leadership. I even helped prepare her for a different role, a role where she was able to then pursue her law degree.

Now she's actually working as a state representative.

She comes to me often and says that I gave her a push and encouragement, a confidence that she didn't have. It was there, but she hadn't tapped into it.

And now? The people in her community are watching her. Young people who never thought someone like them could become a state representative are seeing her and thinking, "Maybe I can do that too."

One person's leap creates ripples that spread further than you can imagine.

LEADING BY EXAMPLE

You don't have to wait until you have everything figured out to start being an example. You don't have to wait until you're successful to inspire others. You don't have to wait until you've made it to give others permission to try.

You lead by example right now, in the middle of your mess, in the middle of your struggle, in the middle of your journey.

Because the people who need your example aren't looking for perfection. They're looking for possibility. They're looking for proof that someone like them can do something hard and survive it. Can take a risk and not be destroyed by it. Can follow a calling and not starve.

Your imperfect journey is exactly the example someone else needs. Your struggle is the proof they're looking for. Your willingness to try even when you're scared is the permission they've been waiting for.

NOT SELFISH, GENEROUS

Here's what I need you to understand: Your transformation is not a selfish pursuit. It's a generous gift.

When you step into your purpose, you're not being self-centered. You're being obedient. And your obedience gives others permission to be obedient too.

When you prioritize your calling, you're not being indulgent. You're being faithful. And your faithfulness shows others what faithfulness looks like.

When you take care of yourself, pursue your dreams, follow God's leading, you're not being selfish. You're being generous with the gift of your example.

So stop apologizing for pursuing your purpose. Stop feeling guilty for taking the leap. Stop second-guessing whether you should be focusing on yourself right now.

You're not just focusing on yourself. You're creating ripples that will touch lives you'll never even know about.

THE INVITATION

So here's what I want you to know: Someone is watching you.

Someone is waiting to see if you'll take the leap. Someone is wondering if it's possible to break the pattern, change the story, try something new. Someone is looking for proof that people like them can do hard things.

And your willingness to go first, even when you're scared, even when you don't have it all figured out, even when people question your choices, gives them the permission they've been waiting for.

Your leap isn't just about you. It's about the ripple effect. It's about everyone whose life will be touched because you were brave enough to follow your calling.

So take the leap. Not just for you. For everyone who's watching and waiting and hoping and praying that if you can do it, maybe they can too.

Be the change. Be the first. Be the example.

The world is waiting for your ripple effect.

REFLECTION QUESTIONS

1. Who in your life might be watching your journey right now? How might your choices be impacting them?
2. Think about someone who inspired you to take a leap. What was it about their example that gave you permission? How can you be that for someone else?
3. If you fully believed that your transformation could spark transformation in others, how would that change your willingness to take risks?
4. What pattern in your family or community could be broken if you went first? What might that make possible for the next generation?
5. How can you reframe your current struggle from "Why is this happening to me?" to "Who might be blessed because I'm going through this?"

TEN

LIVING IN YOUR PURPOSE

What Life Looks Like on the Other Side of Fear

Do you remember how this journey started? With you sitting in your car, unable to bring yourself to walk into work. Or lying awake at 3 AM, staring at the ceiling, wondering if this is really it.

That restlessness you felt wasn't a problem. It was a roadmap. And if you've made it this far through this book, I'm willing to bet you're finally ready to follow it.

But before you take that leap, I want to paint you a picture. Not of some fantasy life where everything is perfect and nothing is hard. But of what's actually waiting for you on the other side of fear. What life really looks like when you stop managing and start leading. When you trade the comfortable prison for the adventurous freedom. When you finally, finally step into the calling God has been whispering to you all along.

Because here's what I've learned after two decades of helping people transform their lives, and after taking my own leap into full-time purpose-driven work: The promised land is real. And it's so much better than you think.

WHEN WORK STOPS FEELING LIKE WORK

There's a question I get asked all the time: "Aren't you afraid to get up in front of hundreds of people? Thousands of people? People from different countries, different industries, different backgrounds?"

And here's my honest answer: No.

I mean, there are still healthy nerves. That moment before you step on stage when you want to do a good job, when you want to honor the people who showed up, when you want to deliver what God called you to deliver. But fear? The kind of fear that makes you sit in your car gathering courage to walk inside? The kind that keeps you up at 3 AM wondering if you made a terrible mistake? That kind of fear? It doesn't live here anymore.

You want to know why? Because I'm living in my purpose. And when you're operating in your purpose, fear doesn't have the same grip on you that it used to.

This is the secret nobody tells you when you're standing at the edge, terrified to jump: The leap is scary. But living outside your purpose is scarier. You just don't realize it yet because you've gotten so used to that particular kind of suffering that it feels normal.

Let me tell you what actually happens when you align your work with your calling:

You wake up energized instead of dreading the day. Even on the mornings when you have a full schedule, when you have challenges to face, when you have problems to solve—you wake up ready. Because the problems you're solving matter. The challenges you're facing are meaningful. The work you're doing is actually moving something forward that's bigger than a paycheck.

I still wake up every morning and ask God: What would You have me do today? Because even when you're aligned with your calling, every day is still a conversation with the One who called you. The plan might look different than what's on my to-do list. The priorities might shift based on what God is showing me that day.

But here's the difference: I'm asking that question from a place of excitement, not desperation. I'm asking "What would You have me do?" not "How am I going to get through this?" That shift changes everything.

Time moves differently. When you're in work that drains you, every hour feels like three. You watch the clock. You count down to lunch, to 5 PM, to Friday, to retirement. Your life becomes a series of things to endure until you can finally rest.

But when you're in your purpose? Hours disappear. Not because it's easy—but because you're engaged. You're present. You're using your gifts instead of suppressing them. You're creating instead of just completing. You're building instead of just maintaining.

Problems feel different. They stop being burdens you have to carry and become puzzles you get to solve. They stop being evidence that something's wrong with you and start being opportunities to grow into more of who you were created to be.

You bring your full self instead of playing a role. You stop code-switching, stop performing, stop pretending to be the person you think you're supposed to be. You just show up as yourself—Southern accent and all, unique perspective and quirky sense of humor and particular way of seeing the world—and it's not just accepted, it's valued. Because it turns out, your authentic self is exactly what your purpose requires.

This isn't just a mindset shift I'm describing. This is what happens when you're finally in the right place. When your gifts align with your work. When your calling aligns with your calendar. When your purpose aligns with your paycheck.

THE MORNING PRAYER THAT CHANGED EVERYTHING

Even now, years into living this purpose-driven life, I start every day the same way. Before I check my phone, before I look at my calendar, before I start solving problems or answering emails, I pray.

And I don't just pray generic prayers. I ask specifically: God, what would You have me do today?

Because here's what I've learned: Even when you're operating in your purpose, you can still drift into managing instead of leading. You can still start optimizing the wrong things. You can still get so busy doing good things that you miss the God things He has for you that day.

That morning prayer keeps me aligned. It reminds me that my business is His business. That my platform is His platform. That my gifts are meant to serve His purposes, not just my preferences.

And when you start your day surrendered like that, when you begin from a place of "Your will, not mine," something shifts. The day unfolds differently. Opportunities appear that you hadn't planned for. Conversations happen that you couldn't have orchestrated. Impact occurs that you couldn't have manufactured.

I want to be intentional about aligning with His will for my life, because that's where true prosperity comes from. Not just financial prosperity—though that comes too when you're operating in your gifts. But the kind of prosperity that means your life is full. Your spirit is satisfied. Your work matters. Your days mean something.

That's the prosperity that lasts. That's the wealth you can't lose in a market crash. That's the security that doesn't depend on someone else's decision to hire you or keep you or promote you.

WHEN GOD'S DREAMS BECOME YOUR DREAMS

I was listening to Oprah Winfrey in an interview recently, and she said something that stopped me in my tracks. She said she prays that she lives out God's dreams for her life.

God's dreams for her life. Not just her own dreams. Not just her own goals. But God's dreams.

And here's the beautiful thing about that: Those dreams align with our deepest dreams. The desires God plants in your heart aren't random. They're not there to torment you or tease you or show you what you can't have. They're there to call you forward. To point you toward the life He designed you to live.

When God plants a dream in your heart, when He calls you to something, it's not going to feel like drudgery once you're actually doing it. Yes, there will be challenges. Yes, there will be hard days. Yes, there will be moments when you have to push through difficulty.

But it's not going to be hard in the way that living outside your purpose is hard. It's not going to be stressful in the way that pretending to be someone you're not is stressful. It's not going to be overwhelming in the way that managing a life that doesn't fit you is overwhelming.

It's a beautiful thing. Because you get to feel a sense of fulfillment that goes beyond just personal satisfaction. You're not only being blessed by it—the people around you are being blessed by it too.

My purpose is to bless and help others reach their goals. I do that in many forms: speaking on stages as a keynote, conducting team trainings, providing one-on-one coaching, writing this book that you're holding in your hands right now.

And I'll tell you, it's inspiring for me to have others grow because of the work we do together. It's invigorating and exciting. When someone tells me they took the leap because of something I said, when someone shares that they finally stepped into their calling after we worked together, when someone breaks through the limiting beliefs that were holding them back—that fills me up. That energizes me. That makes even the hard days worth it.

That's what living in your purpose looks like. Impact becomes inevitable because you're operating in your gifts. Joy becomes your default setting because you're doing what you were created to do. Fulfillment becomes automatic because you're living out God's dreams for your life, and those dreams align perfectly with the deepest desires of your heart.

THE CHECK I STILL HAVE TO DO

Now, I need to be honest about something. Even when you're living in your purpose, you're still human. You still have to manage your ego. You still have to check yourself.

Sometimes, right before I speak to a large audience, I feel those nerves I mentioned earlier. And in those moments, I have to check where my focus is. Because it's easy to slip into making it about me. About my performance. About whether I'm good enough, polished enough, impressive enough.

About whether people will like me. Whether I'll get booked again. Whether I'll look foolish. Whether I'll forget something important. Whether I'll live up to expectations.

But when I catch myself going there, I remind myself: It's not about me. It's never been about me. It's about the calling God has on my life. It's about what He has for me to share with the people He's placed in my path today.

It's about the woman in the third row who's been praying for permission to take her leap, and something I say today will be the confirmation she needed. It's about the man in the back who's been managing his life instead of leading it, and this message will help him see the difference. It's about the person watching the livestream from another country who God specifically arranged to hear this message at this moment because it's exactly what they needed to move forward.

When you shift from "How am I doing?" to "Am I being obedient to what God called me to do?", everything changes. The nerves transform from anxiety into anticipation. The fear transforms into holy expectation. The pressure transforms into privilege.

God is aligning your gifts and your talents with His purpose for you. And that alignment? That's where the magic happens. That's where fear loses its power. That's where you stop performing and start serving.

That's where you realize you're not trying to prove anything to anyone. You're just being obedient. And obedience, it turns out, is so much easier than performance.

THE LIFE YOU BARELY DARED TO IMAGINE

Let me tell you what my life looks like now, years after taking that leap into full-time entrepreneurship. Years after quitting the government job with the six-figure salary and the excellent benefits and all the markers of conventional success.

I travel. Not just for work, though I do speak around the country and internationally. But I travel for joy. I set a goal to visit fifty states by the time I turned fifty, and I'm doing it. I've seen landscapes I never would have seen. Met people I never would have met. Had conversations that expanded my worldview in ways that staying comfortable never could have.

I took my husband to Kenya on a mission trip—his first time in Africa, the continent he'd dreamed of visiting his entire life. And it wasn't just a vacation. It was ministry. It was impact. It was using my gifts and my platform and my resources to bless others while experiencing something transformative ourselves.

I got to spend the last year of my mother's life really being present with her. We went to Orlando—something she'd always wanted to do. We went to Aruba together, multiple times. We had weeks and weeks where I could just be home in Virginia with her, not because I'd carefully hoarded vacation days, but because I'd built a life with flexibility.

When she was in the hospital that final week, I was there. I didn't have to choose between being with her and keeping my job. I didn't have to calculate how much leave I had left or whether I could afford to take unpaid time off. I could just be present for one of the most important weeks of my life.

And after she passed, I could stay home for months. Not rushing back because my bereavement leave ran out. Not forcing myself to show up and perform when I was still grieving. Just being with my family, processing the loss, honoring her memory, and giving myself the space to heal.

Entrepreneurship gave me that flexibility. Purpose-driven work gave me that freedom.

But it's not just about the flexibility, as wonderful as that is. It's about waking up every day and knowing that what I'm building matters. That the conversations I'm having are changing lives. That the coaching I'm doing is giving people permission to step into callings they've been circling for years. That the keynotes I'm delivering are creating ripple effects I'll never even know about.

It's about getting messages from people I've never met telling me that something I said gave them the courage to quit the job that was killing them. Or start the business they'd been dreaming about. Or have the difficult conversation they'd been avoiding. Or finally, finally take the leap they'd been too afraid to take.

That's what's waiting for you on the other side of your fear. Not a life without challenges—I still have those. Not a life without hard days—those happen too. But a life where the challenges matter and the hard days are in service of something bigger than a paycheck.

A life where you're not just surviving until retirement. You're building something that will outlive you.

THE ENERGY SHIFT EVERYONE NOTICES

After two decades of helping leaders find their authentic voice and step into their purpose, I can tell you this: There's nothing more beautiful than watching someone make this shift.

The energy change is palpable. You can see it in their posture—they stand taller, move differently, take up space in a way they never did before. You can hear it in their voice—there's a confidence there that wasn't there before, not arrogance, but groundedness. You can feel it in the room when they walk in—they bring a different energy, a kind of magnetic presence that draws people in.

The impact is exponential. Because when you're operating in your gifts, you're not just more productive—you're more effective. You're creating the kind of value that can't be measured on a spreadsheet. You're solving problems others can't solve because you're bringing your unique combination of gifts, experiences, and perspective.

The joy is infectious. When someone is truly living in their purpose, it makes everyone around them want to find theirs too. Joy becomes contagious. Purpose becomes magnetic. Transformation becomes inevitable because people see what's possible and think, "If they can do it, maybe I can too."

I see this in every person I coach who finally steps into their calling. The entrepreneur who was underpricing her work because she didn't believe she was worth more—after we work on confidence and pricing strategy, she raises her rates and discovers that the right clients gladly pay them. The executive who was managing instead of leading—after they step into authentic leadership, their team transforms. The person who was stuck in a job that drained them—after they take the leap, they can't believe they waited so long.

When you're operating in your sweet spot, that intersection of your gifts, your passion, and the world's need, you don't have to force results. They flow naturally from who you're becoming.

WHAT SUSTAINS A PURPOSE-DRIVEN LIFE

Now, I don't want to paint a picture that's all sunshine and ease. Living in your purpose is the best decision you'll ever make, but it requires some things from you. Let me share the principles that sustain a purpose-driven life—things I've learned from my own journey and from watching hundreds of others live into their calling.

First, purpose-driven living requires ongoing surrender. You don't find your purpose once and then coast. You wake up every day and ask, "God, what would You have me do today?" You stay in conversation. You stay surrendered. You stay teachable. Because the moment you think you've arrived is the moment you start drifting off course.

Second, purpose-driven living is others-focused. If your purpose is just about you feeling fulfilled, you'll burn out. But when your purpose is about serving others, blessing others, helping others step into their gifts, you'll never run out of fuel. The more you pour out, the more you're filled up. It's a paradox, but it's true.

Third, purpose-driven living requires boundaries. Just because you love what you do doesn't mean you should do it all the time. Rest is holy. Sabbath is sacred. Self-care isn't selfish—it's strategic infrastructure. You can't pour from an empty cup, even when you're pouring out of purpose. I still take four vacations a year. I still get my

nails done before big speaking engagements. I still protect time for my family, my health, my relationships. Purpose-driven work is sustainable only when you build sustainability into the system.

Fourth, purpose-driven living means growth never stops. You're always learning, always expanding, always being stretched. But it's the good kind of stretch —the kind that makes you stronger, not the kind that breaks you. You're reading, taking courses, finding mentors, joining communities of people who are where you want to be. You're feeding your mind in the direction you're going. You're investing in yourself because you understand that you're your most valuable asset.

Fifth, purpose-driven living creates a legacy. You're not just building a career or making money. You're building something that will outlast you. You're impacting people who will impact others. You're creating ripples that will continue long after you're gone. That's why my marriage matters beyond just my happiness. That's why my business matters beyond just my income. That's why this book matters beyond just my platform. It's all part of a legacy, a contribution, a way of being the hands and feet of Jesus in the world.

ADDRESSING THE FEAR YOU HAVEN'T SAID OUT LOUD

I know what you're thinking right now. I've coached enough people through this process to know what fear sounds like, even when it's not spoken out loud.

You're thinking: "This all sounds amazing, Teesha. But what if I take the leap and I fail?"

Let me ask you something: What if you don't take the leap and you succeed at building a life you don't even want?

What if you climb the ladder for the next twenty years only to discover it was leaning against the wrong wall the whole time? What if you play it safe and secure and comfortable, and you get to the end of your life and realize you never actually lived it?

Here's what I've learned: The people who regret their choices aren't the ones who tried and failed. They're the ones who never tried at all. They're the ones who played it safe and then spent decades wondering "what if."

You know what failure actually looks like? It's not taking the leap and having to adjust course. That's not failure—that's learning. That's growth. That's how you build the spiritual muscle memory that sustains you through bigger leaps later.

Remember, I tried to move to Atlanta in 2006 and it didn't work. I was there for four days and went back home. By conventional standards, that was a failure. But you know what? It wasn't. It was a training session. It showed me what I needed to work on, what I needed to develop, what gaps I needed to fill before I was ready to sustain that leap.

And eight years later, when God said it was time again, I was ready. Same calling, same destination, different outcome. Because I had built the courage muscle. I had developed the infrastructure. I had surrounded myself with the right people. I had created the spiritual and practical foundation that could support that leap.

The 2006 attempt wasn't wasted. It was preparation.

That's what real failure looks like: staying in the boat. Letting fear win. Choosing comfortable misery over uncomfortable growth. Spending your whole life wondering what could have been if only you'd been brave enough to try.

THE PROMISED LAND IS REAL

Let me paint you one more picture before we finish this journey together.

Five years from now, you took the leap. You stepped into your purpose. You trusted God to catch you, and He did—though not always in the ways you expected. Sometimes He caught you by giving you exactly what you prayed for. Sometimes He caught you by giving you something better than what you imagined. Sometimes He caught you by letting you struggle just enough to build the strength you'd need for what came next.

What does your life look like?

You wake up energized, even on Monday mornings. You do work that matters, that uses your gifts, that makes a difference you can see and feel. You earn income doing things that fill you up instead of drain you. You have flexibility to be present for the people and moments that matter most.

You look back on the comfortable prison you escaped and you can't believe you stayed so long. You see people you've inspired taking their own leaps—your children, your friends, people you've never met who were watching from a distance. You discover gifts you didn't know you had because you were too busy trying to fit into someone else's definition of success.

You pray differently. Not "God, get me through this day" but "God, what would You have me do with this opportunity?" Not "God, help me endure" but "God, help me steward this blessing well."

You rest differently. Not the exhausted collapse of someone who's depleted, but the satisfied rest of someone who's poured out their gifts and seen them multiply. You sleep deeply because your conscience is clear and your life is aligned.

You relate differently. You're not performing for approval or managing impressions. You're just being yourself—quirks and Southern accent and unique perspective and all—and it turns out that's exactly what your purpose required.

This isn't a fantasy. This is the actual lived experience of everyone who's taken the leap and stayed the course. This is my life now. And it can be yours too.

The promised land is real. And you're closer to it than you think.

YOUR COMMISSIONING

This final chapter isn't just information. This is your commissioning. This is your official sending into the calling God has placed on your life.

Because you weren't meant to just read about transformation. You were meant to live it.

You weren't created to spend your whole life wondering "what if." You were created to step into the fullness of who God designed you to be.

Think back to Chapter 1, when we talked about that restlessness you feel. That knowing that there's something more. That sense that you're operating at 50 percent capacity while your real gifts gather dust in a corner somewhere.

That restlessness was your roadmap. And every chapter since then has been equipping you to follow it.

You've learned to recognize the safety trap—how staying comfortable is actually the riskiest choice you'll ever make. You've discovered the five-second leap—that critical window between knowing and doing where courage either wins or fear does. You've started rewriting your story—releasing the limiting narratives you inherited and claiming the truth about who you're called to become.

You've built your courage muscle—understanding that bravery isn't a personality trait, it's a skill you develop through practice. You've fired your limiting board of directors and hired voices that champion your calling. You've shifted from managing to leading—from maintaining what is to creating what could be. You've built your launch pad—the systems and infrastructure that support sustainable transformation.

You've seen the ripple effect—how your leap gives others permission to fly. And now you understand what life looks like on the other side of fear.

You're ready.

Maybe you don't feel ready. But remember: courage isn't the absence of fear. It's taking action in the presence of fear. It's doing the thing even when your hands are shaking and your voice is trembling and your logical mind is listing all the reasons this won't work.

The world is waiting for what you have to offer. Not what you think you should offer. Not what someone else told you to offer. What you were uniquely created to bring.

There are people who need exactly what you have. Problems that need exactly the solution you can provide. Spaces that need exactly the gifts you carry. Children who need to see someone like you doing something extraordinary. Communities that need the change only you can bring. Organizations that need the leadership only you can provide.

But they can't access any of that until you take the leap.

So this is me, giving you the final push. This is me, standing at the edge with you, holding your hand for just a moment before you step out onto the water. This is me, saying what Peter heard all those years ago: "Come."

THE QUESTION THAT CHANGES EVERYTHING

I'm going to leave you with the question I ask myself every morning. The question that keeps me aligned, surrendered, and focused on what actually matters.

God, what would You have me do today?

Not what does my calendar say. Not what do other people expect. Not what would make me look successful or impressive or like I have it all together.

What would You have me do?

Because when you ask that question and actually listen for the answer, everything changes.

You might discover that the leap you're being called to isn't as big as you thought. Maybe it's not quitting your job tomorrow—maybe it's having a conversation, sending an email, signing up for a class, booking a call with a coach.

Or you might discover that the leap is bigger than you imagined. Maybe it's not just about changing jobs—maybe it's about becoming the first in your family to break a generational pattern. Maybe it's about using your pain to heal others. Maybe it's about building something that will outlive you.

But you won't know until you ask. And you won't move until you listen.

So ask the question. Every morning. Every time you face a decision. Every moment you feel that familiar restlessness rising up.

God, what would You have me do?

And then—here's the crucial part—do it. Quickly. In those five seconds before fear builds its case. With the faith that if God did it before, He'll do it again. With the understanding that you don't need to have everything figured out, you just need to take the next step.

Pray. Prepare. Pivot.

That's the framework that's guided every major transformation in my life. That's the pattern that's helped hundreds of people I've coached step into their callings. That's the roadmap that will take you from restless to fulfilled, from managing to leading, from comfortable prison to adventurous freedom.

The life you're meant to live is waiting.

Your purpose is ready.

Your calling is clear.

The world is holding its breath, waiting for you to finally step into who you were always meant to be.

So what are you waiting for?

Let's go.

REFLECTION QUESTIONS

1. When you imagine yourself living fully in your purpose five years from now, what specifically do you see? Write it down in vivid detail—what you're doing, who you're serving, how you feel when you wake up, what your days look like.

2. What's the very first step you need to take this week to move toward that vision? Not the perfect step or the complete plan—just the next small action.

3. Who can you tell about your leap to create accountability and support? Who will champion you, not question you?

4. Complete this sentence: "I will regret it more if I never try, because..." What would it cost you to stay where you are?

5. When you're on the other side of this leap, looking back at this moment, what will you be most grateful you had the courage to do? What will you wish you'd done sooner?

6. Write down your answers. Date them. Keep them somewhere you can find them when doubt creeps in—because it will. And when it does, when fear tries to talk you back into the comfortable prison, pull out these answers and remember: You were made for

more than this. And the restlessness you feel? It's not a problem. It's a roadmap.

7. Follow it.

www.ingramcontent.com/pod-product-compliance
Lightning Source LLC
LaVergne TN
LVHW051004080826
845145LV00009B/2444

* 9 7 8 1 9 6 9 8 2 6 7 0 2 *